Competent Workplace
COMMUNICATION

Analyzing, Developing, Evaluating

Amber N.W. Raile

Dr. Raile is an Assistant Professor and
Director of Business Communications Curriculum in the
Jake Jabs College of Business & Entrepreneurship at
Montana State University.

Kendall Hunt
publishing company

Kendall Hunt
publishing company

www.kendallhunt.com
Send all inquiries to:
4050 Westmark Drive
Dubuque, IA 52004-1840

Printed in the United States of America
10 9 8 7 6 5 4 3 2 1

Contents

PREFACE

Regardless of the field in which you work or the position you hold, most of you will spend the majority of your workday communicating. This communication may include composing emails to your manager, interacting with customers through your company's social media profiles, or giving presentations to large audiences of colleagues. Because most workplace communication situations do not come with explicit instructions or detailed information on how others will evaluate whether you did a "good" job or not, learning how to analyze situations and develop communicative behaviors that are likely to be evaluated positively should be a central part of a business communication course.

This book introduces a competent workplace communication framework rooted in research-based concepts that are easily internalized. To this end, it presents a process for approaching communication situations through acronym-based guidance on being a competent communicator. Rather than focusing primarily on how to write and format a memo, this text takes a choice-based approach to workplace communication, focusing on providing frameworks for making decisions about messages. Using these models of the communication process equips business communicators with the information they need to make decisions about communication. In other words, the text provides the tools to consider your options, information on how to organize the message you need to send, and formatting examples comparable to those provided in other texts.

This approach makes this text unique. Most business communication texts focus on detailing specific prescriptive "how-to" instructions rather than a framework to aidin thinking about how to approach communication situations. The traditional approach of business communication texts focuses on prescribing specific techniques using outdated transmission models of the communication process. Such texts break up their chapters along different writing formats, with chapters for job seeking and presentation skills at the end. However, many of our most complicated communication issues do not arise when presented with a clear format requirement.

Thus, this text does not follow the medium-based approach that other business communication textbooks follow. Formatting in a particular medium is a secondary concern. The first six chapters focus on contextualizing research-based frameworks summarized by acronyms; the last three chapters act as media-specific guides. Woven into each chapter are useful recommendations and process ideas based on research findings. All frameworks are meant to be easily internalized so that they can be helpful as you think through "real-life" situations in the future, without having to reference a text. In short, this text focuses on equipping you with the tools to become a competent communicator—one who understands and is understood.

On a personal note, I would like to acknowledge the support I received from many people while writing this book. From Kendall Hunt Publishing, Kimberly Elliott encouraged me to create my own text to meet my needs, and Beth Trowbridge guided me through the process and kept me on track. My colleagues in the Jake Jabs College of Business & Entrepreneurship trusted me to develop this new approach to how we teach our students about professional communication. I am especially grateful to Stew Mohr, Mike Shaw, and Martha Joh Reeder, who offered their expertise as MSU business communication instructors to provide feedback. My family ultimately provided the support I needed to finish this book. In particular, my parents shared their "real-world" expertise to help improve my content and refine my ideas. Most of all, I am grateful to my husband, who has always been willing to review every important document I write, and my sons; all three of them gave me hugs and accepted many weekends without me so that I could get this project done. I am so fortunate to have this great community who contributed in many different ways.

Part 1

The Importance of Competent Communication

Adapted image © VLADGRIN, 2014. Used under license from Shutterstock, Inc.

Chapter 1
The Role of Communication

Chapter Objectives

After reading this chapter, you should be able to:

- Understand the central role communication plays at work.
- Articulate why theory is useful in addressing real-world situations.
- Recognize the weaknesses of transmission models of communication.
- Identify the benefits of the communication as constitutive approach.

A Vital Workplace Skill

Regardless of the career path you take, you will likely spend most of your day doing one thing: communicating. Communication skills are the only skill set consistently required across almost every single position and job classification.[1] That communication will take many forms. In a given day, you will spend approximately 28% of your time emailing, 19% of your time searching for information, and 14% of your time communicating and collaborating with your colleagues.[2] Communication is prevalent in our lives outside the workplace as well; in total, the average American spends nearly 11 hours each day engaged in communicative activities.[3]

Time spent interacting with others only increases as you move up in an organization or move outside a traditional hierarchy.[4] Managers spend around 90% of their day communicating.[5] CEOs report spending around 85% of their time communicating in meetings, on phone calls, and at public events.[6] Given that the average employee sends and receives an average of 105 emails per day[7] and typical employees spend over a quarter of their time[8] managing email, a considerable amount of the 15% of time CEOs spend alone might be spent on email. If you strike out on your own, communication will still take up most of your time; entrepreneurs spend between 64 and 82% of their time communicating—mostly face-to-face or via email.[9] Regardless of where your career path leads, you are likely to spend a majority of your time communicating.

Not surprisingly, communication skills top the list of qualities employers seek when hiring. Repeatedly, the importance of communication skills is highlighted in surveys of employers and educators alike.[10] Four of the top 10 skills sought by employers are communication related. The top two skills employers look for when hiring are (1) the ability to communicate with internal and external audiences and (2) the ability to work in a team—both of which consistently rate above technical knowledge related to the job.[11] Your ability to write is related to your overall communication abilities, but it is often identified as a separate skill, which is also one of the top 10 skills employers seek. Think about it: your writing ability is often measured before anyone from an organization meets you through your résumé and application materials. A survey of business college deans, who frequently interact with the organizations that employ their graduates, found that writing is one of the top skills employers want.[12] So, communication skills are essential in getting a job.

Once you are hired, you should not be surprised to learn that communication skills play a central role in your continued success given the daily necessity of communicating in many forms. Executives overwhelmingly rate communication skills as the most valuable trait in employees.[13] Your coworkers also want you to have these skills. A national survey of American workers found that 87% of respondents rated communication skills as highly important in the workplace.[14] Over 60% of salaried employees working with large American organizations are required to do some writing in their jobs, and over half of companies consider writing skills in promotion decisions.[15] The Global Talent 2021 report[16] predicts that communication skills—particularly interpersonal skills—will continue to be vital in the future. Further, these skills are broadly defined. A recent content analysis of popular press magazines revealed six competencies required for business communication: (1) relationship and interpersonal communication; (2) mediated communication; (3) intergroup communication; (4) communication of enthusiasm, creativity, and entrepreneurial spirit; (5) nonverbal communication; and (6) speaking and listening.[17] In short, these "soft" skills are essential to your success in getting a job and growing your career. Communication skills are vital in the workplace because "language…empower(s) people to work together to accomplish practical things."[18]

A Skill in Need of Improvement

Communication education is emphasized for a number of reasons, but especially because it contributes to both personal and organizational success.[19] Are you convinced yet? No matter the kind of work you choose to pursue or how many career changes you make, your communication skills will contribute to your hirability and career success. However, employers also consistently report that many college graduates lack these key abilities.[20] Survey after survey suggests that there is a considerable gap between the level of communication-related skills employers seek and the level that potential employees are bringing to the job market. This gap appears to begin even before college; about 75% of high school students fail to demonstrate proficiency in writing.[21] Globally, employers report that a lack of communication-related competency in the applicant pool is often an issue in filling positions through hiring and promotion.[22] Organizations see this gap in communication-related skills as more problematic than the commonly cited gap in technical skills.[23] In other words, though improved technical skills are needed, organizations report that communication skills are in even more serious need of improvement.

Because communication plays a central role in both individual and organizational success, a lack of communication competency can seriously harm careers and organizations. For individuals, bad habits that fall under the umbrella of communication skills—including poor email communication, bad body language, poor grammar or inappropriate word choices, lack of engagement with others, and speaking without thinking—are cited as things that can cost you your job.[24] At the organizational level, poor communication has been cited as a root cause for catastrophic organizational events such as the BP oil spill[25] in the Gulf of Mexico, and a minor typo (a missing "s") kept a bill ending work furloughs for air traffic controllers from being signed by the United States President in May 2013. Our communication missteps with colleagues, employees, managers, customers, and the public risk time, money, resources, opportunities, and even lives.

If you are already a competent communicator, by building on those skills you will make yourself more employable and develop the abilities needed for promotion into leadership roles within an organization. Most of us need work in at least one area—writing research reports, giving constructive feedback, or presenting to large audiences, for example. This book focuses on building your communication competence regardless of where your strengths and weaknesses lie. The secret to building your competence as a communicator is not simply lots of practice (though that will help). To be successful, you need to learn what competent communication looks like. The secret, therefore, might surprise you: practice based on research-tested theory.

Theory?

Your first reaction to hearing that you are going to learn about theory is probably comparable to what most people think when they hear the word "theory." Something like: "But, communication is a skill. Why do I need to learn theory—isn't that ivory tower, useless, and boring?" Try to keep an open mind and frame theory differently in your head. Think of theory as a lens that will forever alter your interpretations of communication situations and your communication behaviors at work (and probably outside of work as well). Theory changes the way you approach ambiguous situations. Many situations and issues you will encounter in your work life will be messy and won't offer time to refer to a "how to" guide. Theories provide frameworks that guide the way you interpret and act in different situations. Understanding a few theories about communication will affect the way you view these situations and give you confidence that you will know how to react.

Theory is useful to us because it has usually been empirically tested with large numbers of people. Theory is not simply someone's opinion of what works, it is something that has been shown to work for many people. Of course, I can't tell you that when Y happens, you should always do Z. I wish I could! Communication is affected by too many factors to be able to know what is always effective all of the time. However, by learning about theory, we increase our chances of effectiveness because we understand what typically works in the situations we encounter. In addition, because the theories we will discuss have been objectively tested, we understand the most likely effects of certain communication behaviors. This approach differs from someone telling you that, based on his experience (i.e., one person's subjective opinion), this *always* works. Maybe it does from his perspective. But, what do the people with whom he communicates think? Using theory to guide your decisions empowers you because it is like relying on thousands of people's aggregated experiences.

Communication as Constitutive

The first theory we will explore together is the meta-theoretical framework scholars use to understand our topic of focus: communication. "Meta-theoretical framework" means that this view underlies the other theories of communication we will discuss in this book; so, understanding this theory is key before we move on to those other theories. Communication skills are important to organizations because communication is what makes (or constitutes) an organization. The "communication as constitutive" framework will help you understand why communication skills are so important to your career success.

A typical business communication textbook uses a "transmission" model of communication that looks something like Figure 1.1.

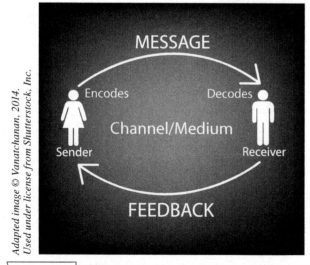

> **Figure 1.1** | A "transmission" model of communication.

This model is not incorrect, but it sure makes it seem like communication is simple. So, this model does help us understand fairly straightforward communication situations, such as scheduling a meeting. A *sender* might *encode* a message in the *medium* of email informing *receivers* about the time and place for a meeting. The *receivers decode* this message and plan to attend. A transmission model adequately captures comparable situations.

However, the transmission model doesn't help us understand communication in more complex situations in a way that helps us to be more competent communicators. Let's play with an example to show why this model is often inadequate. Imagine you want to talk with your manager about applying for a promotion. You are the sender. You schedule a private meeting and enter your manager's office at the designated time. You encode your message in some spoken words. Your message is received by your manager.

> **Figure 1.2** | The "transmission" model in action.

The problem with this model is that it tends to trick us into a simplistic view of the communication process that is not necessarily inaccurate but might lead you to some inappropriate conclusions that affect how others see you. This model typically leads people to think that whatever message they send is transferred into the mind of the recipient(s)—to the extent that you can overcome interference or noise in the channel. Our everyday experiences tell us that this is not how communication works. Other people do not understand messages in an identical way to how we intend them.

Let's return to the conversation with your manager for a moment. Think about it. How might your boss hear this message? What other factors might influence that interpretation? No matter how complex we make the transmission model, it does not capture that this interaction is not the first you have had with your manager. It does not situate your conversation in the organizational context appropriately. It does not help you to understand how your choices affect the direction of this interaction.

Figure 1.3 | Adding complexity to the "transmission" model.

If you approach this conversation with a transmission understanding of how the communication process works, you will probably leave feeling pretty good. On the basis of your manager's response, you believe that you successfully transmitted your message. However, from a constitutive perspective, this interaction was a missed opportunity. We will return to this after a little more discussion of the constitutive model of organizational communication.

The constitutive model conceptualizes communication as a dynamic "process that produces and reproduces shared meaning."[26] Such a model sees communication as a "means by which human beings coordinate actions, create relationships, and maintain organizations."[27] This view of communication seems more consistent with our everyday experiences and interactions. Communication is the force that develops, maintains, and changes our sense of ourselves, our relationships with others, the organizations in which we work, and even the countries in which we live. Communication is not a way to put your ideas into another's head—that's a mind meld!

So, how do the messages we exchange shape organizations? Well, because organizations are extremely complex, no single communication or interaction defines or constitutes them.[28] Instead, multiple interactions over time shape and reshape organizations. The "communication as constitutive of organizations" approach articulated by two communication scholars[28] highlights four communicative flows, which we might think of as processes or topics that structure and restructure organizations. Considering these flows will help you understand in more concrete terms how communication processes shape (or constitute) organizations:

1. Membership negotiation: The process of bringing members into the organization and forming relationships with them is communicative. Employees are recruited and then socialized to "learn the ropes" of the organization and their role in it. However, no employee brings the same skills to a role or performs a role's tasks in a way that is identical to other employees. Thus, both members and organizations are shaped through this continued communication process. Each new employee changes the organization, and the organization changes each new employee.

2. Self-structuring: The process of describing employee roles and tasks is interactive. This structuring might manifest itself as an organization chart showing who reports to whom or in an organization's policy and procedures manual that describes the rules and processes an organization follows. Though such documents might seem to be unchanged and straightforward examples of the transmission model of communication, we know from our own experiences that not everyone "reads" a policy as meaning the same thing. Our different understandings are checked and reframed through discussions with our colleagues. Our view of our role in the organization and the roles of others are shaped through communication as well. In addition, rules, procedures, and roles all change over time through this communication process. Even something that seems very prescribed and straightforward is, in reality, a complex, constitutive process.

3. Activity coordination: An organization's ultimate reason for being is to achieve its goals. These goals are diverse; for example, an organization's

goal might be to produce a product for customers to buy, to share new ideas, or to persuade others to work toward a cause. Multiple individuals or groups are often required to achieve that goal or those goals. Thus, communication is needed to connect work tasks among groups. This communication is often what first comes to mind when we think of what we might learn in a business communication course: emails, meetings, and conference calls, for example.

4. Institutional positioning: Organizations exist within a larger community of customers, suppliers, competitors, partners, communities, and governments. Communication with these stakeholders outside of the organization is necessary for organizational survival and success. We might think of these interactions as marketing, advertising, public relations, or lobbying. The essence of these relationships is communication, and this communication, like the three other forms of communication discussed above, shapes and reshapes organizations. An advertisement that offends consumers affects a company's activity coordination, for example. Thus, this type of communication also constitutes an organization over time.

Returning to the example conversation with your manager, the constitutive lens allows us to see this conversation differently. This interaction is not a chance for you to transmit your decision to your manager but is rather a membership negotiation and self-structuring opportunity. Together in this interaction, you two are shaping your role and the perception of how you fit within the larger organization. From this perspective, this interaction is a missed opportunity to work with your manager to negotiate expanded responsibilities. Further, you have potentially alienated your manager, with whom you will continue to work. If you had approached the interaction as an opportunity to negotiate your role on the team and in the organization, your communication might have been different. Rather than trying to transmit your application to another position, you might have sought to discuss your career path with your manager—potentially leading to a more desirable outcome.

To summarize, communication constitutes organizations through the continuous, simultaneous, and complementary processes of recruiting and socializing new members, defining procedures and organizational structures, coordinating efforts to realize organizational goals, and interacting with stakeholders outside of the organization. Without communication, organizations would not be able to work through these processes.

One More Time: Why Study Communication?

The real power of communication is not the ability to get a job, keep a job, or be successful in a job. The reason that communication is powerful and that its importance is universally recognized in the business world is because communication is constitutive. It shapes our experiences, our interpretations, our organizations, and even how we define ourselves. Communication is powerful because it forms and continually re-creates our experience of the world and how we see ourselves in it. By increasing your competency as a communicator, you will be more effective in shaping your work life and the work lives of those around you in a positive fashion.

Viewing organizations in this way makes it easier to understand why the manner in which you communicate is important and why organizations look for communication skills in employees they hire, retain, and promote. The first three parts of this book focus on providing theory-based information in a practical, applicable manner. Parts 1–3 provide frameworks you can easily memorize and background information you can reference to apply in any communication situation. The information in Parts 1–3 can be used no matter what kind of message you need to communicate. The goal is to help you think through your communication in a specific way. Specifically, we will explore the following:

- Characteristics of competent communicators (Chapter 2)

- Frameworks for analyzing the situation and evaluating your communication (Chapter 3)

- Considerations for choosing the appropriate method or medium for communication (Chapter 4)

- Process models for structuring your communication embodying competent communicator characteristics (Chapter 5)

Part 3 concludes by summarizing all of this information as a process in Chapter 6. Part 4 shifts focus to media-specific concerns. Unlike Parts 1–3 in which all information is relevant to any type of message, Part 4 offers tips for improving your interactions when you choose to talk face-to-face, share information via email, or craft a company-wide memo. Specifically, Part 4 provides information about the following:

- Communicating orally (Chapter 7)
- Communicating electronically (Chapter 8)
- Communicating in traditional forms of business writing (Chapter 9)

Taken together, this book is meant to serve as a guide for the lifelong process of improving your communication competency.

Key Chapter Takeaways

- Communication is a vital workplace skill that can be learned.
- Many prospective and serving employees lack the level of communicative skill sought by employers.
- Communication is more than just sending and receiving messages.
- Communication is a complex, dynamic, and contextual process.
- Misunderstandings are likely to occur because no two individuals see the world alike.
- Communication creates and re-creates our views of self, our relationships with others, and organizations themselves.

Endnotes

[1] Kasper, H. T. (2004, Fall). Matching yourself with the world of work: 2004. *Occupational Outlook Quarterly, 2–21*. Retrieved from the U.S. Bureau of Labor Statistics website: http://www.bls.gov/opub/ooq/2004/fall/art01.pdf

[2] Chui, M., Manyika, J., Bughin, J., Dobbs, R., Roxburgh, C., Sarrazin, J., & Westergren, M. (2012, July). *The social economy: Unlocking value and productivity through social technologies.* Retrieved from the McKinsey & Company website: http://www.mckinsey.com/insights/high_tech_telecoms_internet/the_social_economy?p=1

[3] U.S. Bureau of Labor Statistics. (n.d.). *American time use survey.* Retrieved from the U.S. Bureau of Labor Statistics website: http://www.bls.gov/tus/charts/

[4] U.S. Department of Labor. (n.d.). *Skills to pay the bills: Mastering soft skills for workplace success.* Retrieved from http://www.dol.gov/odep/topics/youth/softskills/

[5] Barrett, D. J. (2006). *Leadership communication: A communication approach for senior-level managers.* Retrieved from https://scholarship.rice.edu/bitstream/handle/1911/27037/Leadership%20Communication%20-%20A%20Communication%20Approach%20for%20Senior-Level%20Managers%20-%20Barrett.pdf?sequence=2

[6] Bandiera, O., Guiso, L., Prat, A., & Sadun, R. (2011). *What do CEOs do?* [Working paper.] Retrieved from the Harvard Business School website: http://hbswk.hbs.edu/item/6662.html

[7] Radicati, S., & Hoang, Q. (2011, May). *Email statistics report, 2011–2015.* Retrieved from The Radicati Group, Inc. website: http://www.radicati.com/wp/wp-content/uploads/2011/05/Email-Statistics-Report-2011-2015-Executive-Summary.pdf

[8] Chui, M., Manyika, J., Bughin, J., Dobbs, R., Roxburgh, C., Sarrazin, J., & Westergren, M. (2012, July). *The social economy: Unlocking value and productivity through social technologies.* Retrieved from the McKinsey & Company website: http://www.mckinsey.com/insights/high_tech_telecoms_internet/the_social_economy?p=1

[9] Mueller, S., Volery, T., & von Siemens, B. (2012). What do entrepreneurs actually do? An observational study of entrepreneurs' everyday behavior in the start-up and growth stages. *Entrepreneurship Theory and Practice,* 995–1017.doi: 10.1111/j.1540-6520.2012.00538.x

[10A] U.S. Department of Labor. (n.d.). *Skills to pay the bills: Mastering soft skills for workplace success.* Retrieved from http://www.dol.gov/odep/topics/youth/softskills/

[10B] Association of American Colleges and Universities. (2005). *Liberal education outcomes: A preliminary report on student achievement in college.* Retrieved from http://www.aacu.org/leap/pdfs/LEAP_Report_FINAL.pdf

[10C] Graduate Management Admission Council. (2011). *Corporate recruiters survey.* Retrieved from http://www.gmac.com/market-intelligence-and-research/research-library/employment-outlook/2011-corporate-recruiters-survey-report.aspx

[11] National Association of Colleges and Employers. (2012, October 2012). *The skills and qualities employers want in their Class of 2013 recruits.* Retrieved from http://www.naceweb.org/s10242012/skills-abilities-qualities-new-hires.aspx?terms=top%2010

[12] English, D. E., Manton, E., & Walker, J. (2007). AACSB College of Business Deans' perception of selected communication competencies. *College Teaching Methods & Styles Journal, 3,* 35–40.

[13] Cline, S. (2005, April 1). Soft skills make the difference in the workplace. Retrieved from the *Colorado Springs Business Journal* website: http://csbj.com/2005/04/01/soft-skills-make-the-difference-in-the-workplace/

[14] John J. Heldrich Center for Workforce Development & Center for Survey Research and Analysis (2000, June). *Making the grade?: What American workers think should be done to improve education* (Heldrich Work Trends Survey, v.2.2). Rutgers, NJ & University of Connecticut.

[15] The National Commission on Writing. (2004, September). *Writing: A ticket to work...or a ticket out. A survey of business leaders.* Retrieved from the College Board website: http://www.collegeboard.com/prod_downloads/writingcom/writing-ticket-to-work.pdf

[16] Towers Watson. (2012). *Global Talent 2021: How the new geography of talent will transform human resource strategies.* Retrieved from http://www.towerswatson.com/en-TH/Insights/IC-Types/Survey-Research-Results/2012/07/Global-Talent-2021

[17] Waldeck, J., Durante, C., Helmuth, B., & Marcia, B. (2012) Communication in a changing world: Contemporary perspectives on business communication competence. *Journal of Education for Business, 87,* 230–240. doi: 10.1080/08832323.2011.608388

[18] Taylor, J. R. (2009). Organizing from the bottom up? Reflections on the constitution of organization in communication. In L. L. Putnam & A. M. Nicotera (Eds.) *Building theories of organization: The constitutive role of communication* (pp. 153–186). New York, NY: Routledge.

[19] Morreale, S. P., & Pearson, J. C. (2008). Why communication education is important: The centrality of the discipline in the 21st Century. *Communication Education, 57,* 224–240. doi: 10.1080/03634520701861713

[20] National Association of Colleges and Employers. (2011, September 14). *College students' communication skills.* Retrieved from www.naceweb.org/printerFriendly.aspx?printpage=/s09142011/communication_skill/

[21] National Center for Education Statistics, U.S. Department of Education. (2012). *The Nation's report card: Writing 2011.* Retrieved from http://nces.ed.gov/nationsreportcard/pdf/main2011/2012470.pdf

[22] Manpower Group. (2013). *2013 talent shortage survey: Research results.* Retrieved from http://www.manpowergroup.com/wps/wcm/connect/587d2b45-c47a-4647-a7c1-e7a74f68fb85/2013_Talent_Shortage_Survey_Results_US_high+res.pdf?MOD=AJPERES

[23] Adecco Group. (2013, September 30). *Lack of soft skills negatively impacts today's U.S. workforce.* Retrieved from http://www.adeccousa.com/articles/Lack-of-Soft-Skills-Negatively-Impacts-Today's-US-Workforce.html?id=218&url=/pressroom/pressreleases/Pages/Forms/AllItems.aspx&templateurl=/adeccogroup/News/press-releases/Pages/press-release.aspx

[24] Smith, J. (2012, October 17). *14 bad habits that can cost you your job.* Retrieved from the Forbes website: http://www.forbes.com/sites/jacquelynsmith/2012/10/17/14-bad-habits-that-can-cost-you-your-job/

[25] National Commission on the BP Deepwater Horizon Oil Spill and Offshore Drilling. (2011, January). *Deep water: The Gulf oil disaster and the future of offshore drilling, report to the President.* Washington, DC:National Commission on the BP Deepwater Horizon Oil Spill and Offshore Drilling.

[26] Craig, R. T. (1999). Communication theory as a field. *Communication Theory, 9,* 119–161.

[27] Putnam, L. L., Nicotera, A. M., & McPhee, R. D. (2009). Introduction: Communication constitutes organization. In L. L. Putnam & A. M. Nicotera (Eds.) *Building theories of organization: The constitutive role of communication* (pp. 153–186). New York, NY: Routledge.

[28] McPhee, R. D., & Zaug, P. (2009). The communicative constitution of organizations: A framework for explanation. In L. L. Putnam & A. M. Nicotera (Eds.) *Building theories of organization: The constitutive role of communication* (pp. 153–186). New York, NY: Routledge.

Your Turn

Name _____

Provide a summary of Chapter 1 in three–four sentences.

What are the most important pieces of information for you in this chapter?

What questions do you still have after reading this chapter?

Chapter 2

A Framework for Competent Workplace Communication

Chapter Objectives

After reading this chapter, you should be able to:

- Articulate the three components of the ADE model for competent communication.
- Identify how different analytical approaches to situations affect communication.
- Recognize the variety of encoding/decoding behaviors needed to develop a competent communication behavior/skill set.
- Follow the ADE process to show competent communication.
- Apply the ADE model to evaluate your own and other's communication.

What Is Competent Communication?

Communication is important, but more communication does not necessarily equal better (or even good) communication. Because communication actively shapes the organizations in which we work, we want to make sure that we are not only communicating but also communicating competently. So, what does it mean to be a competent communicator? Many popular press articles about "good communication" point to messages that share information, feelings, or opinions effectively[1] in a "clear, credible, authentic way."[2] Such characterizations do little to help us know how we can improve our communication.

Research on competent communication paints a similar—yet substantively different—view of good communication. We typically judge others' competence as communicators by what they say or write (verbal cues) and how they say or write their messages (nonverbal cues). However, this observable behavior is only one, albeit important, piece of the puzzle. Competent communication relies on multiple factors, some of which are not directly observable. Increasing your own competence as a communicator turns out to be more about understanding communication situations and expanding your options for acting within them.

Figure 2.1 illustrates the ADE (analyze, develop, and evaluate) model for communication competence. Competent communication involves analyzing your options, developing a behavioral/skill repertoire, and evaluating your performance. Each

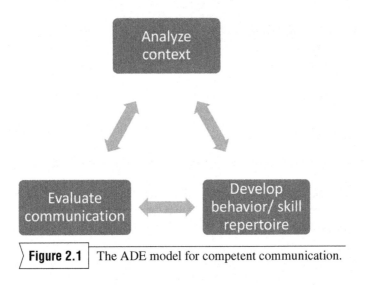

Figure 2.1 | The ADE model for competent communication.

aspect is mutually dependent and related to how you and others will assess your communication. Remember, no matter how "competent" you or others find your communication to be, your communication with others is worthy of continued improvement.

Competent Communication: Analyzing

Competent communication starts with cognition—or thinking—about communicating. Competent communications share certain mental characteristics. Do not be tempted to think of these as traits with which you were born; think of them as characteristics you can develop. Expanding your personal view of communication and learning underlying theories about communication is a perfect way to develop these mental characteristics. Specifically, competent communicators tend to be good at the related activities of perspective taking, self-monitoring, and showing cognitive complexity. Perspective taking means they are able to see the situations from the point of view of another person. Self-monitoring means that they can reflect on their own behaviors and how they are received. Though self-monitoring is sometimes considered to be a personality trait (i.e., someone is either a high self-monitor or a low self-monitor), we can condition ourselves to be more reflective about our own behavior in communication situations. Cognitive complexity is the "mental ability to distinguish subtle personality and behavior differences among people."[3] A cognitively complex person is a sophisticated observer and is able to anticipate other's reactions and adjust communication accordingly.

People who are higher in cognitive complexity tend to see situations differently and tend to recognize the need to tailor their message to the situation and the people in it. Therefore, individuals might approach communication situations in very different ways. Consider how you view communication situations. Think for a minute about what the purpose of communication is. Which of the following descriptions best captures how you view communication most of the time?

1. I communicate to share my thoughts. Communication is the way we tell other people what we think.

2. Certain situations require you to say certain things. I typically try to say what is appropriate in the situation.

3. Through what I say and how I say it, I can shape the way people see situations. I am very strategic in how I choose my words.

The way people view communication affects their communication behavior and effectiveness in achieving their goals. The idea is that we grow and develop in our understanding of communication and become increasingly sophisticated in how we "use" communication (i.e., our message design logic). Most research shows that people tend to rely on one type of design logic at a given point in their lives. Message design logics[4] says that our view of communication as (1) expressive, (2) conventional, (3) or rhetorical affects our effectiveness as a communicator and the creativity of our messages.

How does our view of communication as expression, convention, or rhetoric affect our messages? An example might help to show how these different message design logics lead to different messages. Imagine a job interview. Candidate 1 (Expressive) would probably talk about what she wants in a job. After all, expression and telling people about yourself is the goal of communication in this orientation. Candidate 2 (Conventional) would likely offer canned answers to the questions (e.g., "My greatest weakness is that I care too much!") because he thinks such responses are expected in the situation. Candidate 3 (Rhetorical) would see an interview as a way to reframe the situation for the interviewer and the organization. The interviewee's focus in the interaction would be on specifically matching her unique skill set to the company's needs to show how she would benefit the company—rather than focusing on how the job would benefit her. Many people tend to approach communication conventionally, meaning they recognize what is appropriate in the situation and follow social norms. Candidate 2 would likely behave appropriately in the interview example but certainly would not stand out. In more complex situations (such as an interview), you can see how a rhetorical response might be evaluated as more competent. As you can see in the table on the next page, a rhetorical message design logic is also most consistent with the communication as constitutive framework introduced in Chapter 1.

Competent communication is partly analytical. Communicators who are seen as competent tend to think about communication in a particular way. Both conventional and rhetorical message design logics take the situation and the people in it into account in communication. Those who combine a rhetorical design logic with higher cognitive complexity will likely show greater behavioral flexibility. The behavioral/skill repertoire of a competent communicator offers many options for message design, resulting in the construction of person-centered messages, which are tailor-made messages crafted for a specific individual and context. Compared to a conventional or expressive design logic, those who view communication with

Comparing the three design logics		
Expressive	**Conventional**	**Rhetorical**
Function of communication is to express what you feel so others understand your thoughts/ behavior	Function of communication is to say what's appropriate according to context and roles	Function of communication is to create and negotiate roles and situations
Clarity and honesty are characteristics of "good" communication	Appropriateness is characteristic of "good" communication	Flexibility and sophistication are characteristics of "good" communication
Context is unimportant	Context determines appropriateness	Context is created through communication

greater flexibility can imagine multiple messages that are appropriate in a given situation. So, how we analyze a communicative situation affects how our communication is viewed by others and our success as communicators.

Competent Communication: Developing a Behavioral Repertoire

The behavioral/skill repertoire of a competent communicator will offer multiple behaviors and skills useful in communication situations. Regardless of the medium you use to communicate (e.g., phone, group meeting, or text message), communication involves a verbal component. In later chapters, these behaviors or skills will be discussed in detail and tips specific to different communication situations will be provided. Of course, competency in each of these areas is characterized by specific behaviors. In broad strokes, these are the four most common verbal communication behaviors in the workplace:

- Information sharing (e.g., explaining, asking questions, giving feedback, and problem solving)
- Relational maintenance (e.g., joking, small talk, and so on)
- Expressing negative emotion (e.g., complaining)
- Organizing (e.g., planning, managing, and scheduling)[5]

Communicators need both encoding and decoding skills[6] to engage in all these types of behaviors. Encoding skills include a keen understanding of language (including grammar and vocabulary), clear verbal expression, appropriate accompanying non-verbals, and efficiency. Decoding skills include attention, active listening, and the ability to respond appropriately to a message. Both encoding and decoding also require cultural awareness. Developing these skills is key to increasing your communication competency; without these skills, your behavior is unlikely to be seen as competent across multiple situations.

Encoding

1) *Understanding of language*

- Sufficient vocabulary: Do you know enough words in the language to convey your message?
- Knowledge of grammatical conventions/rules: Do you use proper sentence construction and follow grammatical rules?

2) *Clear verbal expression*

- Message clarity: Do you choose words that are readily understood by your co-communicator(s)?
- Message content: Do you provide enough information to allow your co-communicator(s) to understand your meaning?
- Message organization: Do you present your message in a logical fashion?
- Message articulation: Is your message communicated with vocal/printed clarity so that your co-communicator(s) can listen to it or read it?

3) *Appropriate nonverbal communication*

- Kinesics (if applicable): Do you use your body to complement your message?
  - Facial expressions
  - Eyes and eye contact
  - Gestures
  - Touch

- Physical characteristics: Do you pay attention to the messages your co-communicators might interpret about the way you present yourself and your message?
  - Personal appearance
  - Document appearance
  - Visual aids
- Proxemics (if applicable): Do you use physical space to complement your message?
- Paravocalics: Do you use qualities of verbal communication separate from your words to complement your message?
  - Pitch
  - Volume
  - Timbre (quality)
  - Resonance (pronunciation)
  - Speech rate
  - Use of fillers and/or pauses
  - Stress or emphasis[7]
- Chronemics: Do you use time to complement your message?
- Aesthetics: Do you use the environment to complement your message?

4) *Cultural awareness*

- Does your message take into account the expectations your co-communicator(s) will have given the setting in which you are communicating?

Decoding

1) *Attention*

- Are you focusing cognitive resources on the complete message (including both verbal and available nonverbal cues)?

2) *Active listening/interpretation*

- Processing: Are you centrally processing (i.e., actively attending to) the message?
- Cues: Are you providing feedback to your co-communicator(s)?

3) *Ability to respond appropriately*
   - Information: Do you have the information or knowledge you need to respond to your co-communicator(s)?
   - Composure: Do you have the emotional control you need to respond to your co-communicator(s)?
   - Context: Does the situation allow for you to provide your response?

4) *Cultural awareness*
   - Does your interpretation take into account the expectations your co-communicator(s) will have given the setting in which you are communicating?

Thinking of your communication skills in these terms reminds us that communication is more than just talking or writing. As co-communicators, we are responsible for creating shared meaning with another person or a group of people. The more skills we have in terms of encoding and decoding, the more likely we are to reach shared meaning with our co-communicators. A competent communicator has a diverse set of behaviors/skills from which the appropriate behavior can be selected and enacted in a particular situation.

Competent Communication: Evaluating

Our communication behavior in a given situation is determined by our cognition (views of communication situations) and selection of appropriate communication behaviors. These thoughts and evaluations both inform and are informed by our interactions with co-communicators. Though cognition and our behavioral repertoire are internal, both can be shaped by reactions and feedback from our co-communicators. Competent communicators examine and consider the reactions of their co-communicators and adapt in the interaction (if possible) or use that feedback to guide future cognition and selection of communicative behaviors. Because they recognize the central role of communication in constituting relationships and organizations, competent communicators carefully consider and evaluate their communication.

Communication that is perceived as competent by others and positively constitutes relationships and organizations results from a continuous interplay of analyzing the situation, developing a behavioral/skill repertoire, and evaluating your performance.

Competent communicators reap the career benefits discussed in Chapter 1—specifically, better chances of being hired and promoted. No matter how "competent" you or others find your communication to be, your communication with others is worthy of continued improvement. After introducing and defining this perspective on competent communication, the next chapter offers standards for evaluating the competence of your own communication and that of your co-communicators.

Key Chapter Takeaways

- Competent communicators understand their options, behave appropriately, and achieve their goals effectively.

- To improve your communication competency, you need to analyze situations, develop your behavioral repertoire, and evaluate your effectiveness (ADE).

- Competent communicators try to take the perspective of others and recognize that, because communication constitutes our experiences, we have choices about how we frame messages and situations.

- Competent communicators select from a variety of encoding and decoding skills to best address the situation.

- Both during and after communication experiences, competent communicators reflect on their behavior, which improves their ability to anticipate and evaluate situational factors and modify behavior accordingly.

- The ADE model can be used for discrete communication situations and as a life-cycle model that can be revisited to improve your communication competence across time.

Endnotes

[1] Ask.com (n.d.). *What is good communication*? Retrieved from http://www.ask.com/question/what-is-good-communication

[2] Tardanico, S. (2012, November 29). 5 habits of highly effective communicators. *Forbes*. Retrieved from http://www.forbes.com/sites/susantardanico/2012/11/29/5-habits-of-highly-effective-communicators/

[3] Griffin, E. (2011). *A first look at communication theory* (8th ed.). City, SS: McGraw-Hill.

[4] O'Keefe, B. J. (1988). The logic of message design: Individual differences in reasoning about communication. *Communication Monographs, 55*, 80–103. doi: 10.1080/03637758809376159

[5] Keyton, J., Caputo, J. M., Ford, E. A., Fu, R., Leibowitz, S. A., Liu, T., & Wu, C. (2013). Investigating verbal workplace communication behaviors. *Journal of Business Communication, 50*, 152–169. doi: 10.1177/0021943612474990

[6] Monge, P. R., Bachman, S. G., Dillard, J. P., & Eisenberg, E. M. (1982). Communicator competence in the workplace: Model testing and scale development. In M. Burgoon (Ed.), *Communication yearbook 5* (pp. 505–527). New Brunswick, NJ: International Communication Association.

[7] Frank, M. G., Maroulis, A., & Griffin, D. J. (2012). The voice. In D. Matsumoto, M. G. Frank, & H. S. Hwang (Eds.), *Nonverbal communication: Science and applications* (pp. 53–74). Los Angeles, CA: Sage.

Part 2

Analyzing Communication Situations

Adapted image © VLADGRIN, 2014. Used under license from Shutterstock, Inc.

Chapter 3

SPACE Considerations

Image © VLADGRIN, 2014.
Used under license from Shutterstock, Inc.

Chapter Objectives

After reading this chapter, you should be able to:

- Explain the meaning of each letter in the SPACE acronym.
- Describe each component of the SPACE framework.
- Outline the considerations of the SAID acronym.
- Recognize basic professional norms.
- Understand how the ADE, SPACE, and SAID frameworks relate to one another.
- Know how to apply the SPACE framework in communication situations.

Understanding Your Communication SPACE

In Chapter 2, we discussed how competent communication involves understanding the constitutive nature of communication (analysis) in a way that allows us to develop multiple behavioral options (behavioral/skill repertoire) before selecting what we expect to be the most effective communicative approach in a particular situation (evaluation and performance). Of course, our co-communicators see only this "performance" and evaluate our communication competence themselves.

By understanding the factors that can be used to evaluate communication competence, we can increase the likelihood both that our communication will be perceived as competent by others and that our communication will be effective. This chapter introduces a framework for analyzing situations, developing messages, and evaluating effectiveness. These characteristics of competent communication pull together everything discussed in the opening chapters of this book and provide a framework for use as you consider your communication and that of others. Though this list is not exhaustive, it captures some key factors that are meant to be useful across situations, messages, mediums, and communicators.

Let's return to the basic considerations we discussed in the first chapter: Why do we communicate? Communication shapes the way we and others see the world and the organizations in which we work. Ultimately, our messages (along with those of our co-communicators) constitute the organizations in which we work. Along these lines, we want to think about competent communication as the result of an understanding of the communication SPACE in which we find ourselves. Competent communication is

- Strategic
- People Centered
- Appropriate
- Correct and Concise
- Ethical

Though our communication with others can take many forms—for instance, written messages ranging from texts to formal reports, oral presentations, team discussions, and interpersonal conversations—these considerations will help you as you work to shape messages that will be evaluated by others as competent. By focusing on these characteristics, we have both a framework and a process with which we can analyze the communication situation to develop a behavioral/skill repertoire from which we can select effective approaches to the situation. We can also evaluate our own communication and that of others using the SPACE framework. Now, I will describe these five characteristics and provide information that we can refer back to as we discuss different types of communication in Part 4.

Strategic

When we view communication as strategic, it is intentionally goal oriented.[1] As individuals, we often judge the success of a particular message or our abilities as a communicator by the degree to which we obtain our goals. When we select communication behaviors to achieve particular results, we are engaging in interactions with others to achieve goals.[2] Some people are upset by the idea that their communication is strategic or goal driven. Often, thinking of our workplace communication as strategic is easier than thinking of our other communication as goal driven. For example, we create a résumé and prepare for interviews with the goal of getting a job. We respond to a client email with the goal of providing helpful information and retaining that client. We prepare a written report for our manager with the goal of being seen as capable in our role. However, without necessarily being conscious of it, we are often pursuing multiple goals through our interactions with others.

Our goals can be described in a number of ways. In addition to being individual, goals may be co-constructed by people in a relationship (like you and your manager) or in a group (like work team or organizational goals).[3] Though one goal might be more important or primary, we typically try to achieve three types of overarching goals[4] simultaneously when interacting with others:

1. Instrumental goals: What specific action, response, and/or resource are you trying to obtain through your communication?

   - We typically focus on these outcome-oriented goals, though they are not necessarily most important.

   - Informative goals and persuasive goals are most common in professional communication.

2. Interpersonal (or Relational) goals: Are you trying to develop, maintain, or end a relationship with your co-communicator(s)?

   - Messages may differ depending on relationship status.

   - Our co-communicators appreciate messages that support how they see themselves and the impression they want others to have.

   - Messages that focus solely on directly serving instrumental goals may neglect relational/interpersonal goals.

3. Identity (or Self-Presentation) goals: How do you want your co-communicator(s) to see you?

   - We want to present ourselves in a way that leads others to respect us as professionals.

   - Messages that focus solely on directly serving instrumental goals may neglect self-presentation/identity goals.

Logically, our goals should affect the behaviors we choose[5] from our behavioral/ skill repertoires. In other words, our communication should vary depending on the goals we are pursuing in a given interaction.[6] However, communication (particularly less competent communication) is not always rational in the sense that we deliberately choose behaviors based on whether they will help us reach our goals in a particular situation.[3] Instead, most people rely on comfortable approaches that have been successful in the past.[7] Competent communicators learn to recognize that the success of a behavior depends on the nature of our interactions and the situation (or SPACE) in which we are communicating. Whether your communication actually achieves your goals is a way you can evaluate its competence (but more on that later).

People Centered

How often have you listened to someone speak or read and wondered: "What's in this for me?" "How does this relate to what I need to know?" "Will this be on the test?" We expect the messages we receive to take us into account. In order to achieve your goals as a communicator, you can take such experiences into account. When someone sends you a message, you want it to be personalized to you and to address your concerns. The people with whom you interact—your co-communicators—will feel the same and will judge your messages based on how well you address their concerns.

Often, you will see references to your "audience" or the "receiver" when talking about communication. Such terms are more consistent with the transmission or sender/receiver model of communication. Because we view communication as constitutive, I use the term co-communicator to put all parties on equal footing. Instead of thinking about someone who passively accepts whatever message you send (i.e., the receiver), think about the other parties as equally responsible and involved co-communicators. Together, you are shaping how each other views the situation, which forces you to give equal consideration to your co-communicator's goals, interests, perspectives, and needs.

Your co-communicator(s) might be determined by your goals, or they might determine your goal. For example, if you are seeking information that a particular person has, your co-communicator is determined by your (instrumental) goal. Conversely, if you are responding to a request from someone else, that co-communicator will determine your goals. Either way, considering your co-communicator is a necessary factor in achieving your goals.

In order to more effectively achieve your goals, your communication should be tailored to your co-communicators—in other words, your communication should be people centered. You might have a single targeted or known co-communicator for a particular message—for example, an email exchange with your colleagues. However, you do not want to overlook other co-communicators—for example, anyone to whom your emails might be forwarded. Thus, we are typically concerned with identifying and considering targeted co-communicator(s) and then considering how others who read or hear about the communication or might be affected by it (i.e., a secondary co-communicator) will perceive the communication. You need to focus your message on the needs of all people who might directly or indirectly become aware of what you say.

In order to be competent in your communication, you need to gather as much information as possible about both your targeted and secondary co-communicators. Both may consist of different people with different needs and expectations. Start by asking yourself:

- With whom am I communicating? (These are your targeted co-communicators.)

- Who else might see my communication? (These are your secondary co-communicators.)

After you identify your co-communicators, you need to consider what should be SAID. In order to do so you need to identify the following:

Situation	How do your goals relate to those of your co-communicators?
	How receptive will your co-communicators be to your goals?
	Are there any threats to your co-communicators' sense of control or self-esteem in this situation?
Attitudes	How might your co-communicators feel about the message you have to convey?
	Does your message threaten your co-communicators' sense of control or their self-esteem?
	What opinions will your co-communicators already have about the situation?
	How might your co-communicators respond to your message?
Information	What do your co-communicators already know?
	What information do you need to provide?
	What misinformation will you have to correct?
Demographics	What are your co-communicators like?
	How might that affect how you choose to communicate with them? For example, are they likely to expect a certain level of formality or to prefer a certain medium?
	Where are your co-communicators located?
	How much diversity in attitudes and information is there?

Considering other people's needs is sometimes referred to as audience analysis. Whatever you call it, understanding your co-communicators is essential for competent communication. Just as you do not speak to the head of your company as you might talk to one of your close friends, learning to focus on the other people in the situation is a key step to being evaluated as a competent, professional communicator. Employ your perspective taking skills (discussed in Chapter 2) to identify others' needs and goals. Then, focus your message accordingly.

Appropriate

Of course, others will typically judge communication competence in business on the basis of whether they feel the message is "appropriate." But, how can we predict ahead of time whether a message will be seen by others as appropriate? Appropriateness is in many ways situationally determined. For example, choosing a face-to-face message rather than an email to convey sensitive information would typically be seen as the more appropriate choice. The chapters ahead cover more specifics about what is likely to be seen as appropriate given the form of communication (e.g., email, face-to-face conversation, and memo) you select. You want to be strategic by identifying your goals (instrumental, relational, and self-presentational) and considering the other people with whom you will interact and their needs. Doing so increases the likelihood that your message will be seen as appropriate.

In addition to being strategic and people-centered, appropriate communication fits the larger context or situation. Particular organizational settings will have different norms (or typical patterns/unspoken rules) about what is appropriate. For example, tech companies might favor tech-savvy forms of written communication over formal memos. Let's consider you and an organization of which you are a member—your university or college. You are probably quite familiar with some norms at your university, such as what is acceptable to wear to class or how to address your professors. If you were to visit a high school friend who attends a different college or university, you might notice differences in what is seen as appropriate at that institution. Until you are aware of the particular views of appropriate communication in an organization, you can follow larger social norms around professionalism.

Presenting yourself and your message professionally and politely (which is how social appropriateness can be defined[8]) is considered appropriate communication in most business settings. For example,

- Formal address: Refer to people by title (e.g., Ms. for women; Mr. for men; or Dr., Prof., or whatever title an advanced degree might afford) until told another form of address is appropriate. Some organizations might be more informal in modes of address (e.g., everyone goes by their first name) than others.

- Business attire: Dress appropriately to convey respect for the situation. You will probably feel more uncomfortable and be seen as less appropriate when you are underdressed versus overdressed.

- Technology use: Avoid using your cell phone, tablet, or computer unless your co-communicator(s) explicitly state(s) that doing so is okay.

- Tact: Show consideration for the other party and the situation in your communication.

- Demonstration of behavioral skills: Develop the behaviors and skills identified in this text.

When planning and engaging in communication with others, we should understand that others will consider appropriateness in evaluating our competence as a communicator. By developing our behavioral/skill repertoires so that we can select communication that fits our strategy, we increase the chances that we will be perceived as competent by our co-communicators. By focusing on the other people in the situation and tailoring our message to their needs, we are more likely to both meet our goals and be seen as appropriate. Competent communicators do not always behave perfectly in a given situation, but they critically consider the situation and learn from their mistakes—correcting them in future communication situations.

Correct and Concise

Your message is more likely to be seen as competent if you are correct and concise. For your message to be correct, you should follow norms and conventions for mechanics (e.g., grammar, spelling, and punctuation), format correctly (e.g., know the difference between a memo and a letter), and present accurate information. If you struggle with grammar, spelling, or punctuation rules, there are a number of written grammar guidebooks, online tools, and apps available to help you practice and develop those skills. Correct mechanics are a baseline expectation for employment. You are unlikely to be hired if your application materials, for example, contain typos. Employers expect you to be mechanically correct in this way. If you feel your skills need further development, identify tools that work for you.

One skill that many of us need to develop in business writing is conciseness, which is matching the level of directness to the situation. A related concept—efficiency—can be defined "as expending the least effort to obtain whatever outcome is desired…from that encounter."[9] Thus, conciseness can be thought of as both succinctness and focus.

- Succinctness: Do you streamline your message to include only vital information?

- Focus: Do you limit your message to a few main points?

Concise communication does not necessarily translate to brevity. Rather, a concise message matches the complexity of the situation. More complex situations might require longer messages. However, messages should retain a focus and succinctness so that they are "just right" for the situation. Working to streamline your communication through revision and editing will help with conciseness. The chapters that follow will offer you specific tips about maximizing efficiency in different forms of business communication.

Ethical

Because competent communicators are other-focused, your concern for your co-communicators weighs heavily on your need to achieve your goals. You cannot achieve relational or self-presentation goals, in particular, if you are dishonest in your communication. The framework outlined here is inherently ethical. Ethical communication involves understanding your goals, considering how you will communicate, and evaluating the outcomes that result from your communication.[10] Both your intentions going into a communicative situation and the actual outcomes determine the ethicality of your communication. Further, presenting information that you feel is credible is necessary, a topic that will be discussed in Chapter 5. A framework for evaluating how ethical your messages are, called the Principle of Veracity, closely matches the ADE framework for competent communication described in Chapter 2. The Principle of Veracity provides four considerations for ethical communication:

1. Consult your conscience for direction. (*Analyze*)

2. Consider your available options. (*Develop*)

3. Ask what your peers would think of your message. (*Evaluate*)

4. Shift your perspective to consider how all co-communicators would view your communication. (*Evaluate*)[10]

As you can see, everything we have discussed thus far about being a competent communicator would pass the tests laid out by the Principle of Veracity. You must analyze your goals and consider your co-communicators before developing your message. Once you engage in the communicative behavior, you and others should evaluate both your communication and its results. Thus, ethical considerations are necessary for competent communication.

Pulling the Frameworks Together

By considering your SPACE and what should be SAID to your co-communicators, you are well on your way in the process of analyzing, developing, and evaluating (ADEing) your communication. Using this framework will help you consciously develop your communication competence. The ethical communication framework discussed in this chapter includes an important component that we did not discuss much—the means through which you choose to communicate. The next chapter introduces a framework for making decisions about the medium through which you will communicate.

Key Chapter Takeaways

- Competent communication is
  - Strategic: Aimed at meeting instrumental/outcome goals, relational goals, and self-presentation goals.
  - People Centered: Informed by the situation, co-communicator attitudes, information needs, and demographics.
  - Appropriate: Matched with goals and co-communicators to communicate the message in a professional, polite manner using appropriate media.
  - Correct and Concise: Presented succinctly using grammar, formatting, and information that are accurate and focused.
  - Ethical: Developed with consideration of the situation, your options, your co-communicators, and your conscience.
- Attuning to SPACE considerations provides a framework for developing your own communication and evaluating its effectiveness.
- Other's communication can also be evaluated using the SPACE framework.

Endnotes

[1A] Berger, C. R. (1997). *Planning strategic interaction: Attaining goals through communicative action.* Mahwah, NJ: Erlbaum.

[1B] Canary, D. J., Cody, M. J., Manusov, V. L. (2000). *Interpersonal communication: A goals-based approach* (2nd Ed.) Boston: Bedford/St. Martin's.

[1C] Kellermann, K. (1992). Communication: Inherently strategic and primarily automatic. *Communication Monographs, 59,* 288–300.

[2] Berger, C. R., & Kellermann, K. (1994). Acquiring social information. In J.A. Daly & J. Wiemann (Eds.), *Communicating strategically* (pp. 1–31). Hillsdale, NJ: Erlbaum.

[3] Wiemann, J. M., & Daly, J. A. (1994). Introduction: Getting your own way. In J. A. Daly & J. Wiemann (Eds.), *Communicating strategically* (pp. vii–xiv). Hillsdale, NJ: Erlbaum.

[4] Clark, R. A., & Delia, J. G. (1979): TOPOI and rhetorical competence. *Quarterly Journal of Speech, 65,* 187–206. http://dx.doi.org/10.1080/00335637909383470

[5] Cody, M. J., Canary, D. J., & Smith, S. W. (1994). Compliance-gaining goals: An inductive analysis of actor's goal types, strategies, and successes. In J. A. Daly & J. Wiemann (Eds.), *Communicating strategically* (pp. 33–90). Hillsdale, NJ: Erlbaum.

[6] Kellermann, K. (2004). A goal-directed approach to gaining compliance: Relating difference among goals to differences in behaviors. *Communication Research,* 31, 397–445.

[7] Berger, C. R. (2008). Planning theory of communication. In L. A. Baxter & D. O. Braithwaite (Eds.), *Engaging theories in interpersonal communication: Multiple perspectives* (pp. 89–101). Thousand Oaks, CA: Sage.

[8] Kellermann, K., Kim, M.-S., & Park, H. S. (2000). *Conversational constraint congruence: Efficiency, appropriateness, and task-oriented goals.* Unpublished manuscript.

[9] Kellermann, K. (1988, March). *Understanding tactical choice: Metagoals in conversation.* Paper presented at the Temple Discourse Conference, Philadelphia, PA.

[10] Makau, J. M. (2009). Ethical and unethical communication. In W. F. Eadie (Ed.) *21st century communication: A reference handbook* (pp. 433–444). Thousand Oaks, CA: SAGE.

Chapter 4

Identifying Your Means of Communication

Chapter Objectives

After reading this chapter, you should be able to:

- Identify different forms of media available for professional communication.

- Explain factors that influence our media choices and others' evaluations of our choices.

- Articulate the characteristics of different media.

- Match characteristics of different media to different types of communication situations.

Deciding What Type of Message to Send

Competent communicators consider their options, choose the best way of conveying their message, and possess the skills to deliver it appropriately and correctly. Though being a "good communicator" may come more naturally to some, everyone can develop the cognitive understanding and behavioral skills necessary to become a competent communicator. Some individuals are naturally inclined to the cognitive and behavioral skills that others need to work to develop. Some of us feel more comfortable communicating in certain situations (for example, talking with a close colleague) than in others (like writing a report for dissemination to your whole organization or giving a formal presentation in front of a large audience).

Because we are more comfortable communicating in certain ways, we sometimes make the mistake of relying on that form of communication across situations. In this chapter, we are going to discuss considerations for choosing a medium with which to communicate. When most people hear the word "media," they think about television or the Internet. While this characterization is not incorrect, we want to think about media more broadly moving forward. A medium is the way you choose to communicate your message. So, while the television or Internet are forms of media, so are emails, face-to-face conversations, text messages, group meetings, written memos, and so on.

Media have traditionally been characterized by researchers in terms of their "richness." Richness can be thought of as the level of social presence felt,[1] the signal-carrying capacity of the medium, or the different types of cues we can use when communicating via that medium. Figure 4.1 is organized by the richness of each medium. Face-to-face is the richest medium because of the plentitude of cues we can communicate face-to-face. We have the words we choose, the vocalics used to say them, the facial expressions we make, and the gestures and body language we use. Compare face-to-face communication to something like a text message, in which we have only the words we choose—often in abbreviated form. The signal-carrying capacity of a face-to-face message makes it a richer medium because we can convey more information using this medium than we can with others.

For a long time, researchers focused on this characteristic of media and assumed it drove our choices as to which medium we chose to communicate a message. Our own experiences tell us this is not necessarily true. In classes, we are not often

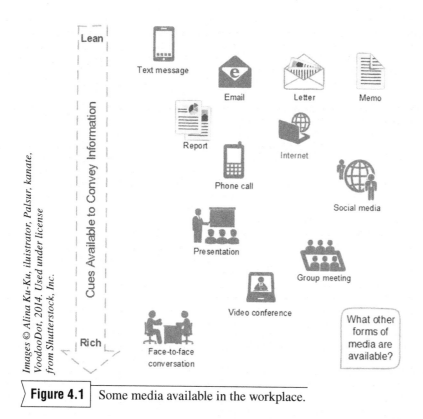

Lean

Cues Available to Convey Information

Rich

Text message

Email

Letter

Memo

Report

Internet

Phone call

Social media

Presentation

Group meeting

Video conference

Face-to-face conversation

What other forms of media are available?

Images © Alina Ku-Ku, illustrator, Palsur, kanate, VoodooDot, 2014. Used under license from Shutterstock, Inc.

Figure 4.1 | Some media available in the workplace.

asked to consider or choose an appropriate medium. Instead, we are assigned to write a report or give a speech. Often, we default to certain media once we are in the "real world" because we have become comfortable with them. For example, we might want to give someone bad news via email rather than face-to-face because we are more comfortable with that medium, rather than because that is the best way to communicate the message. Our personal experiences drive our media choice just as much as the objective characteristics of a particular medium.

You might not get to transfer your skills in choosing an appropriate medium in your college coursework (mainly because it can be difficult for your professors to compare your outputs in different mediums). However, you can practice these choices in your personal life, current work, or extracurricular commitments. For example, if you need to give bad news to someone, how should you do that? In this chapter, I provide considerations to help with making decisions about important messages you need to communicate—both inside of and outside of the workplace. Considering the first two components of the SPACE model (i.e., strategy and people) will help you identify what is appropriate and ethical in terms of media choice. Of course, specific skills and behaviors are needed for you to appear competent when communicating in different forms of media and will be discussed in Chapters 7–9.

The Social Information Model of Media Use in Organizations

Again, we are going to turn to a theoretical framework to help us gain understanding of what the analysis of media choice should involve. In other words, what should we consider when planning to communicate a particular message at work? Keep in mind that competent communication is judged both by our effectiveness in achieving our own goals and through positive evaluations by our co-communicators. Thus, the considerations we need to make when communicating a message are related both to our own needs (strategic, goal-based) and to the needs of our co-communicators (people centered).

In organizations, we might be particularly concerned with what our coworkers, managers, and other stakeholders view as appropriate. We gather information from our workplace interactions, observations, and experiences to determine what is viewed as an appropriate medium choice. The social information model of media use in organizations[2] explores how our own experiences, others' influence, the organizational context, and the "richness" of a particular form of media affect our choices about how we will communicate. After discussing this model, I will combine it with the considerations of a competent communicator to develop some guidelines you can use to select an appropriate medium for a message.

The social information model of media use in organizations acknowledges that, though media might have objective characteristics (such as "richness"), we do not make choices about media use objectively. The model itself is complex, so I will present a modified version of it visually (Figure 4.2) and provide explanation of its components.

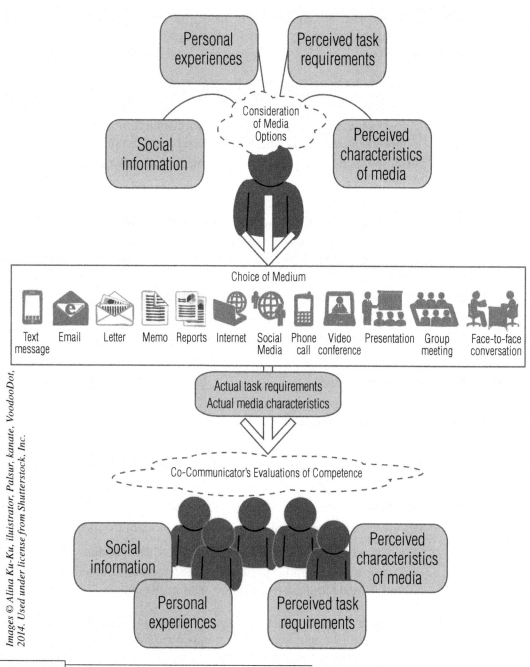

Personal experiences

Perceived task requirements

Social information

Consideration of Media Options

Perceived characteristics of media

Choice of Medium

Text message | Email | Letter | Memo | Reports | Internet | Social Media | Phone call | Video conference | Presentation | Group meeting | Face-to-face conversation

Actual task requirements
Actual media characteristics

Co-Communicator's Evaluations of Competence

Social information

Perceived characteristics of media

Personal experiences

Perceived task requirements

Figure 4.2 Making choices about media in organizations.

In essence, the idea is that our use of media (or our choice to use a particular form of media) and others' evaluations of that choice are affected by the following factors:

- Social information (attitudes we perceive others to have about a medium)
  - Gathered by observing others' behaviors and listening to their statements
  - Examples: organizational culture; information from and opinions of coworkers, managers, clients, etc.; social norms; contextual cues
- Personal experiences (previous uses of media and performances of tasks)
  - Gathered by evaluating our own experiences and analyzing the current task requirements
  - Examples: attitudes about the medium and the task, knowledge of the medium and the task, past behaviors related to the medium and the particular type of task, and reactions of others to use of medium for particular tasks
- Perceived task requirements (what we think the task is)
  - Gathered from directions from others and our ideas about the task, including whether the task and message are:
    · Ambiguous/open to interpretation?
    · Confidential?
    · Requiring documentation?
    · Time sensitive?
    · Lengthy?
  - Examples: job descriptions; requests from others; previous tasks; information from and opinions of coworkers, managers, clients, etc., about the task
- Perceived characteristics of media (what you think of the media options)
  - Gathered from previous use of media and other's previous uses of media
  - Examples: comparative level of richness/presence afforded by media options and familiarity or comfort with media options

Of course, these factors interact with one another and influence perceptions of media choice. For example, some clear trends regarding appropriateness of different forms of media for addressing certain tasks have arisen. Sensitive tasks that involve personal, confidential, or critical messages are perceived as most appropriately communicated through face-to-face conversation. Conversely, routine, nonconfidential, or noncritical messages are more appropriately communicated through email.[3] So, evaluating these factors independently is not sufficient; these considerations should inform a holistic view of the communicative situation.

Let's explore this model through an example. Imagine that you need to assign an employee a new job task. You work at a company that values using email as a form of communication for its efficiency. Your employees (including this employee) tend to respond quickly to email and access their accounts nearly all hours of the day using their smart phones. Thus, the social information you gather favors the use of email for most tasks. Due to the organizational environment, you typically use email to assign tasks to employees. You have a favorable view of email as a form of communication with your employees and understand well how to use it. So, your personal experiences with the medium predispose you to using it. You feel the task at hand is quite straightforward and well suited to email. Finally, you feel that words on a screen are sufficient to convey your message. Thus, you are very likely to choose email to assign an employee a new job task over the other options (like a face-to-face meeting, a phone call, a memo, a text message, etc.).

However, walking through these steps does not necessarily mean that your chosen medium (in this case, email) is indeed the best choice because our perceptions of the social environment, our previous experiences, the task, and the medium are not always accurate. In this example, many of the times you choose to use email to assign a new task, email will be an appropriate choice. However, if your employee is new, if the task is more ambiguous than you might suspect, or if the email system at your company has been experiencing glitches that might prevent your employee from actually receiving the message, email might not be the "best" medium. The model is not concerned with whether the choice is appropriate, however. The model is concerned with how you make the choice and assumes that this all happens fairly automatically.

I wanted to describe this model you to help you understand how we make choices about our medium and how we can sometimes make mistakes. We can make serious errors if we misread the nature of the task; rely too much on our own attitudes, knowledge, and experiences; or misread the social environment. In an organization, these errors can be amplified. We have all heard stories in the news about employees fired via email or managers who have sent out difficult messages via internal website announcements. These are clear examples of the stakes. People typically do not pay much attention to our choice of medium until we make the wrong choice—one that violates the norms at our organization or strikes people as inappropriate to the communication task at hand.

Characteristics of Different Media

In Figure 4.2, you can see that your choices will be compared with both fairly objective characteristics of media and your co-communicators' perceptions of the medium you chose to communicate. Though perceptions are important, I want to focus now on the characteristics of different forms of media.

Admittedly, the list in Figure 4.3 does not encompass all media options available, but it captures fairly common ones within organizations. These types of media are divided into three categories: (1) traditional written media, (2) electronic media, and (3) oral media. You can see this figure incorporates factors of the social information model of media use in organizations by identifying particular task/message considerations, co-communicator considerations, and characteristics of media.

- Level of verbal detail: Certain media lend themselves better to detailed, lengthy verbal messages than others. In addition, some social information or commonly accepted practices will affect the preferred length of messages in certain media. More straightforward, simple tasks can make use of media in which shorter messages are expected.

- Nonverbal cues available: A big area of difference across media is "richness" or signal-carrying capacity. More straightforward, simple tasks can make use of media with fewer nonverbal cues.

- Number of co-communicators: The number of people with whom you are communicating will make particular forms of media more appropriate than others.

- Asynchronous?: A distinguishing characteristic among different forms of media is whether or not the co-communicators involved in the interaction need to be simultaneously (i.e., synchronously) interacting or whether they can send messages at different times (i.e., asynchronously).

- Level of privacy: Media differ in the level of confidentiality they provide to co-communicators.

Channel	Medium	Level of Verbal Detail (Length)	Nonverbal Cues Available	Number of Co-Communicators	Asynchronous?	Level of Privacy	Permanence	Interaction Speed/ Immediacy	"Redo" Capability
Traditional Written *Best when:* • Permanent record needed • High level of detail required • Formality desired	Letter	1–2 pages	Appearance, Tone	Small (1)	Yes	Mod	High	Slow	High
	Memo	< 3 pages	Appearance, Tone	Varies	Yes	Mod	High	Slow	High
	Report	> 3 pages	Appearance, Tone	Varies	Yes	Mod	High	Slow	High
Electronic *Best when:* • Message needs to be delivered quickly • Privacy is not required • Level of detail needed is low • Feedback is desired, but immediacy is less important	Text message	1 screen	Type Cues (e.g., font, emoticons)	Small	Yes/ No	Low/ Mod	Mod	Varies	Mod
	Email	1 screen	Appearance, Tone, Type Cues	Varies	Yes	Low	High	Varies	High
	Internet	1 screen	Varies	Varies	Yes	Low	High– Mod	Varies	High
	Social media	Varies	Varies	Varies	Yes/ No	Low	High	Varies	High
Oral *Best when:* • Message requires rich cues, immediate feedback • No permanent record needed • Interaction can be synchronous • Message can be delivered without need to edit	Phone call	Varies	Paravocalics	Small	No	High	Low	Fast	Low
	Presentation	Varies	Kinesics, Appearance, Proxemics, Paravocalics, Chronemics	Varies	No	Mod	Varies	Mod	Low
	Group meeting	Varies	Kinesics, Appearance, Proxemics, Paravocalics, Chronemics	Mod (3–10)	No	Mod	Varies	Fast	Low
	Video Conference	Varies	Kinesics, Appearance, Paravocalics, Chronemics	Small	No	High	Low	Fast	Low
	Face-to-face conversation	Varies	Kinesics, Appearance, Proxemics, Paravocalics, Chronemics	Small (1)	No	High	Low	Fast	Low

> **Figure 4.3**   Media characteristics.

- Permanence: Some forms of media offer the opportunity to preserve messages better than others.

- Interaction Speed/Immediacy: Related to synchronicity, some media offer the chance to modify your message during the interaction on the basis of co-communicator behavior or interests.

- "Redo" capability: Particularly when used asynchronously, some forms of media offer more opportunity to work through (and get feedback on) multiple drafts for delivery.

Obviously, I cannot provide a magical model that will prevent you from ever making a mistake in choosing your medium. (Sorry. Keep reading. I promise I still have some good stuff to share.) What I can do is remind you that awareness and analysis are key skills of a competent communicator. Those who consider the factors outlined in the social information model of media use in organizations when planning their message are more likely to be perceived as competent. Competent communicators consider many factors as they carefully plan their message. Factors like these are given attention even before a message is planned or drafted, which we turn to in the next chapter.

Key Chapter Takeaways

- Multiple forms of media (including oral, electronic, and traditional written) are available for workplace communication.

- These forms of media vary in the number of cues they offer for sending messages, which is sometimes called "richness."

- Most of the time, we consider a number of factors—including available social information, our personal experiences, and our perceptions of the communication task and the media available to enact it—when selecting a medium we will use to communicate.

- Media differ in the level of verbal detail and nonverbal cues available; synchronicity; levels of privacy and permanence; interaction speed or immediacy; and opportunities to work through multiple attempts at delivering the message.

- Characteristics of situations—like the size of the audience—make some forms of media more suitable.

- Media choice should be carefully considered, not done out of habit or comfort.

Endnotes

[1] Short, J. A., Williams, E., & Christie, B. (1976). *The social psychology of telecommunications*. London: John Wiley & Sons.

[2] Fulk, J., Steinfield, C. W., Schmitz, J., & Power, J. G. (1987). A social information processing model of media use in organizations. *Communication Research, 14*, 529–552.

[3] Kupritz, V. W., & Cowell, E. (2011). Productive management communication: Online and face-to-face. *Journal of Business Communication, 48*, 54–82. doi: 10.1177/0021943610385656

Part 3

Developing and Evaluating Competent Messages

Chapter
5

Structuring Your Message

Chapter Objectives

After reading this chapter, you should be able to:

- Understand how to use the SPACE model to identify key points.
- Know the different types of sources you can gather.
- Use the ABCs to evaluate your sources
- Recognize that you need to cite your sources using a proper set of guidelines (such as APA style).
- Choose a direct or indirect approach based on the communicative SPACE.
- Convert your key points and resources into an outline following a direct or indirect approach.
- Apply the house model to form strong arguments at both the macro (whole message) and the micro (sections or paragraphs) levels.
- Select the most effective message sidedness strategy for a given SPACE.

An Iterative Approach to Structuring Your Message

After thinking about your goals, co-communicators, and medium, you can identify message strategies that demonstrate an understanding of your communication SPACE. Your message should be targeted based on what you want to achieve, with whom you are communicating, and with what you choose to communicate. The most effective message strategies for business communication map to these considerations. Though the communication process might appear to be linear, the illustration of the ADE model from Chapter 2 shows that this is actually an iterative process (i.e., "arriving at a decision by repeating rounds of analysis...to bring the desired...result closer to discovery with each repetition")[1] of organizing and information gathering. This chapter will lead you through the specifics of developing a message, but you will recognize that completing these steps in this order is not always required. In developing a message, you might revisit previous steps or jump ahead. Depending on your communication task, you might mix and match these steps. Even if you do proceed linearly through this process, you might go through it several times for one communicative task. Though for simplicity this process is presented to you as a series of steps, always keep in mind that this process is meant to be iterative. This chapter serves as an overview of and guidance for one potential iterative process.

Information Strategy: Identifying Key Points

Organizing your thoughts is an often-skipped—but vital—step in the communication process. Organizational techniques serve as the basis from which you generate your message. The SPACE framework is an effective way of pulling together what should be SAID, your goals, and media considerations. You can identify your goal(s), summarize your co-communicator analysis, evaluate your media options, and characterize concerns related to the organizational context in which you are communicating. Too often, we start writing or speaking only to be tripped up because we have not taken the time to think about our message. Our communication lacks conciseness when it is not clearly focused around our goals. Further, our message might be viewed as inappropriate because it does not fit the situation.

Clearly, organizing our thoughts prior to communicating them is a key step as we aim for competent communication.

You should start with the SPACE information you identified in your planning. Your goal (e.g., to inform your colleagues of an upcoming meeting) translates nicely into a topic statement. Based on this, consider the key piece or pieces of information you want to share with your co-communicators. For example, if you are planning to inform your co-communicators about an upcoming meeting, you might need to provide the date, time, location, and agenda for that meeting. Or, the meeting could be a standing meeting for which those details are unimportant. You might instead need to convince your co-communicators to prepare by reading a particular document or completing particular tasks prior to the meeting. Thus, the key points you want to make are given in the table as follows:

Goal/Topic statement: Inform of upcoming meeting	Goal/Topic statement: Inform of work/Persuade to complete
Key Points: 1. Reference upcoming meeting 2. List attendees 3. Identify date, time, and location 4. Provide agenda	Key Points: 1. Reference upcoming meeting 2. Identify work to be completed 3. Convince of importance of work 4. Provide agenda

Information Strategy: Research

Identifying your key points or claims reminds you of the kind of information you need to gather to support them. Of course, relatively simple scenarios (like these meeting scenarios) may not require much formal research. However, more complex situations will likely require additional support. Research involves collecting all of the information needed not only to make your claim but also to refute counterarguments to your claim.

How can you research? Typically, we think about research in terms of primary and secondary sources. Primary sources are ones you gather yourself. For example, you might conduct a survey of your coworkers to learn their views on a particular issue. You might interview someone who is an expert on the topic you wish to discuss. You might collect original documents—like emails or memos—about the topic and draw conclusions on the basis of their reading. All are examples of primary sources; you are gathering the data and drawing conclusions. Conversely, secondary sources generally provide conclusions for you. If you access an analysis or research project conducted by someone else, you are gathering a secondary source. With secondary sources, you must trust the interpretation or analysis of the authors or researchers.

Whether you gather primary or secondary sources to support your claims, you need to evaluate the quality of those sources. Many different guidelines for assessing the quality of your sources exist. However, many of them are similar to those provided by the Montana State University Library.[2] Keep in the mind their ABCs for understanding the strengths and weaknesses of your primary and secondary sources.

A. Authority
- Does this person/group know what they are talking about?
- Use sources only when you can clearly identify the author.
- Assess whether the author's credentials provide expertise in the topic. (Does the author have an advanced degree or exceptional experience in the topic area?)
- Learn more about the organization if a source is group-authored.

B. Bias
- Is the source objective?
- Is it all opinion or are there facts? How can you tell?
- Evaluate whether more than one side of an issue is represented.
- Consider whether the author/group has a clear stake in the issue or stands to benefit from its stance in a tangible way.
- Evaluate the quality and nature of the evidence provided to support the claims made.

C. Content

- Is the information useful or relevant to my topic/claim?
- Identify what the source adds to your outlined main topics.
- Judge whether the source provides new information related to your topic.

C. Currency

- Is the information timely?
- Check the publication or posting date.
- Decide whether the information provided is likely to be outdated.

Because you aim to be correct, concise, and ethical in your communication, the ABCs of evaluating information are vital. You are responsible for the quality of information you use to support your claims. The challenge is finding the right balance to be strategic, people focused, appropriate, correct and concise, and ethical in your argument.

One additional consideration for ethical communication that also strengthens the quality of your argument is citing your sources. Source citation improves the ethicality of your messages because you are appropriately crediting the ideas of others. You are also offering the opportunity for your co-communicators to learn more about the topic themselves because citations tell them how to access the information you reference. Your content is strengthened by citing your sources because your co-communicators will understand that the claims you make go beyond just your opinion. Including the expertise of others (who happen to support your claims) makes your argument even stronger. For these reasons, you need to cite any sources you use to create your message. Each organization wil l have its own rules or norms for how to cite sources. Many business schools, for example, follow the guidelines set forth by the American Psychological Association (APA). Ultimately, the act of consistently citing your sources following a set of guidelines, such as APA's, is necessary to be a competent communicator.

Organizing Strategy: Direct vs. Indirect Message Organizations

Once you consider the SPACE and gather information on the main topics you need to cover, you can turn your attention to developing your message. A primary consideration is how your co-communicators might react to both your goals and your content. You need to figure out if what should be SAID fits better with a direct or indirect approach.

A direct approach presents the main idea right away. The key points you wish to make will be clearly outlined in the first paragraph. The direct approach is more appropriate when

- your co-communicators are unlikely to disagree with or be opposed to the information you present (for informative goals)
- your co-communicators will agree with or are unlikely to feel strongly opposed to what you are recommending (for persuasive goals)
- your co-communicators prefer a direct approach
- your co-communicators are likely to overlook your key points if not presented directly[3]
- your co-communicators' self-esteem is unlikely to be affected by the key points
- your co-communicators' sense of autonomy or choice is unlikely to be affected by the key points

Conversely, an indirect approach contextualizes the message but reserves the main points until your co-communicators have the appropriate information to interpret your message. A key guideline for using the indirect approach is consideration of how your message will affect your co-communicators. Specifically, the indirect approach is more appropriate when

- your co-communicators are likely to disagree with or be opposed to the information you present (for informative goals)
- your co-communicators will disagree with or are likely to feel strongly opposed to what you are recommending (for persuasive goals)

- you plan to present a logical argument that builds to your recommendation, key point, or goal[3] (for persuasive goals)
- your co-communicators are likely to devote time and focus to your message
- your co-communicators' self-esteem is likely to be affected by the key points
- your co-communicators' sense of autonomy or choice is likely to be affected by the key points

To illustrate, let's return to the more complex of the two meeting goals.

Goal/Topic statement: Inform of work/Persuade to complete

Key Points:

1. Reference upcoming meeting
2. Identify work to be completed
3. Convince of importance of work
4. Provide agenda

Now, imagine two different communicative SPACEs for that goal. In Scenario 1, email is the preferred form of communication in your organization and is one you favor for tasks like scheduling a meeting. Your co-communicators are unlikely to disagree with or be opposed to your request. Because the project is a top priority for everyone at the meeting, your request that they complete their work prior to the meeting is unlikely to threaten their self-esteem or their sense of control. Thus, you plan to take a direct approach to your email. In Scenario 2, email is also the preferred form of communication in your organization and is one you favor for tasks like scheduling a meeting. However, in this situation, your co-communicators are feeling pressed for time. This project is a priority for you, but it is only one of many things the others in this work group must do. You risk appearing critical of their time management or directive about how your colleagues should prioritize their work. Thus, you decide to take an indirect approach in your email because of potential threats to self-esteem or autonomy. So, the same task may require different approaches, depending on the context.

Organizing Strategy: Outlining

Once you have decided whether you will use a direct or indirect approach, you can expand your key points to plan your message. A traditional approach to organizing or planning your message is an outline. An outline is a useful way to organize your thoughts for anticipated communication across all forms of media. The formality of the outline can vary depending on the communication task at hand. For example, if you have decided to use email, you likely have a relatively short, straightforward task; thus, the outlining process would be fairly quick and informal. The outline would serve as a check to ensure that your goals are likely to be achieved because you have considered the information your co-communicators needed and provided it appropriately, correctly and concisely, and ethically. For a longer document, presentation, or important conversation, an outline becomes even more vital. In some cases, like a group meeting or face-to-face conversation, this outline will serve as a guideline for you as you manage this complex interaction, incorporating your co-communicators' interpretation of your message and any information they share with you.

All formal communication (meaning the kind addressed in this text) follows a basic pattern: introduction, body, and conclusion. Further, the same kind of information tends to be included in the introduction, body, and conclusion. This pattern should be followed regardless of the medium used or length of the message (Figure 5.1).

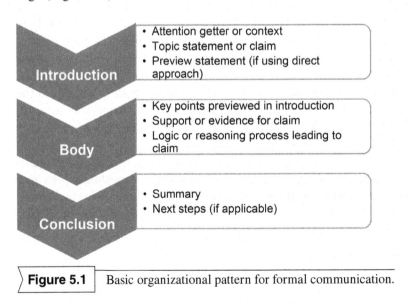

Introduction
- Attention getter or context
- Topic statement or claim
- Preview statement (if using direct approach)

Body
- Key points previewed in introduction
- Support or evidence for claim
- Logic or reasoning process leading to claim

Conclusion
- Summary
- Next steps (if applicable)

Figure 5.1 | Basic organizational pattern for formal communication.

You can generate your outline around this basic structure. An outline provides a flexible format for developing the key points by helping to identify supporting content around which you can create a paragraph or section (depending on the medium you have selected). Under each main point, you can identify supporting information to share. Further, your outline allows you to organize your key points based on your selection of an indirect or direct strategy.

Let's return to the two scenarios we constructed for your more complex meeting goal. In Scenario 1, you planned to take a direct approach to your email. Your outline would look something like the one shown in Figure 5.2.

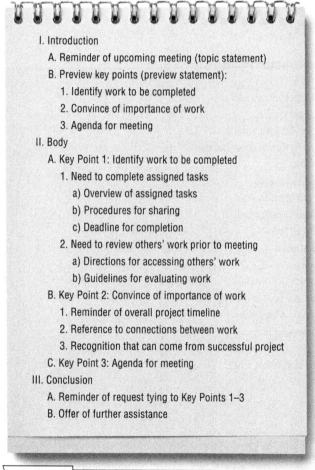

I. Introduction
   A. Reminder of upcoming meeting (topic statement)
   B. Preview key points (preview statement):
      1. Identify work to be completed
      2. Convince of importance of work
      3. Agenda for meeting
II. Body
   A. Key Point 1: Identify work to be completed
      1. Need to complete assigned tasks
         a) Overview of assigned tasks
         b) Procedures for sharing
         c) Deadline for completion
      2. Need to review others' work prior to meeting
         a) Directions for accessing others' work
         b) Guidelines for evaluating work
   B. Key Point 2: Convince of importance of work
      1. Reminder of overall project timeline
      2. Reference to connections between work
      3. Recognition that can come from successful project
   C. Key Point 3: Agenda for meeting
III. Conclusion
   A. Reminder of request tying to Key Points 1–3
   B. Offer of further assistance

Figure 5.2 | Example direct message outline.

In Scenario 2, you decided to take an indirect approach in your email because of potential threats to self-esteem or autonomy. Keep in mind, the key points you need to cover are the same in both scenarios. However, the organizational structure you outline will differ. To take an indirect strategy, as shown in Figure 5.3, you contextualize the information before providing direction or making a recommendation.

Thus, developing a rough outline helps you keep your key points at the forefront while fleshing out the details you need to make your case. An outline structures your message based on all of the information you have gathered about your communication situation.

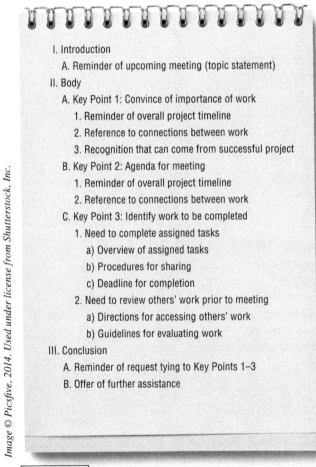

Figure 5.3 Example indirect message outline.

Information and Organizing Strategy: Logical Arguments

Often, to achieve our goals, we need to present a persuasive case—or an argument—to our co-communicators. Many people have negative associations with the word "argument." As used here, an argument is not a dispute or just stating your opinions; an argument is an "effort to support certain views with reasons."[4] Arguments are logical, and logic turns out to be a consistently effective persuasive tactic in general[5] and in organizations especially.[6] So, how do you create a logical argument? Here is an approach that can be used across contexts to communicate a logical, persuasive argument.[7] The most basic form of this model provides three building blocks for making an effective argument:

- Claim: States goal or an assertion that supports our goal.
- Grounds: Includes specific forms of evidence that support the claim.
- Warrant: Specifies why the grounds support the claim.

We will use a metaphor to make sense of this model: a house (see Figure 5.4).

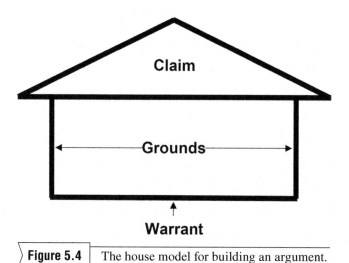

| Figure 5.4 | The house model for building an argument. |

This model helps us remember the information we need to include in our message to make an effective case and achieve our goal. The claim is represented by the roof. Everything under the roof is part of the house; correspondingly, everything in our message should be related to the goal or assertion made in the central claim. The grounds are represented by the walls. Just as the walls of a house support its roof, the grounds should support your claim. The warrant is represented by the foundation. The foundation (warrant) ties everything together—connecting the roof (claim) and the walls (warrant). Without a solid foundation, the walls and roof will be unstable. This metaphor provides an easy-to-remember way to structure your communication.

Further, this simple model can be applied to arguments at multiple levels of complexity. You might be planning a message with one overarching claim: for example, a message calling for increasing the salaries of entry-level positions.

1. Identify the argument you want to make to your co-communicators.

   Salaries should be higher in our entry-level positions. (Claim)

2. Consider the evidence or details that your co-communicators need to support that claim.

   The company's salaries are lower than those of competitors. (Grounds)

   Internally promoted employees are better performers than those externally hired for upper-level roles. (Grounds)

   Employees who enter through entry level-roles and are promoted are less likely to leave. (Grounds)

3. Connect your evidence to the claim you made.

   Attracting and retaining good entry-level employees is important to the organization; higher salaries would help us do both. (Warrant)

At the macro argument level, your claim often becomes a thesis statement in your introduction. You will have numerous forms of evidence (grounds, each in its own body section) to support that claim. In a direct approach, each form of evidence will be identified in the preview statement in your introduction and will have its own paragraph in a written document. For example, you might argue that your salaries are lower than those of your competitors, that those who are internally promoted are better performers than those externally hired for upper-level roles, and that employees who enter through entry-level roles and are promoted are less likely to leave the organization. This evidence will be connected to your central claim through a warrant. For example, you present these forms of evidence because you think attracting and retaining good entry-level employees is important to the organization. The warrant is key to the argument; if you present evidence without explaining how it supports your claim, your co-communicators might not make the connection that you intend. Help your co-communicators (and yourself) by specifically using a warrant to connect the evidence that you provide to the claim you are making.

At the more micro (section or paragraph) level, these three components can be used to develop each individual piece of evidence. For example, you claim that employees who are internally promoted are better performers than those hired externally. To support this claim, you might present two forms of evidence (or grounds): comparative performance review data for both internal promotions and external hires and comparative sales numbers for both groups. Again, the warrant is vital. If performance review data and comparative sales numbers are not seen as valid indicators of performance, your claim that internally promoted employees are stronger performers than external hires will not be supported. If your co-communicators value team players and external hires are consistently evaluated higher on team skills, your claim will fall flat.

This structure also works for informative goals because people tend to be receptive to logic. Let's apply this model to the task of informing our team about an upcoming meeting.

1. Identify key point/information you want your co-communicators to know.

   Our team will meet this week. (Claim)

2. Consider the evidence or details that your co-communicators need to support that claim.

   The team will need to know the location of the meeting, date, time, meeting agenda, expected outcomes, etc. (Grounds)

3. Decide whether to connect that information to the key point. (Compared to persuasive goals, warrants for informative goals might be unspoken.)

   This information will help all team members to attend and participate effectively in the meeting. (Warrant)

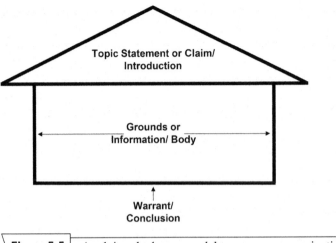

Figure 5.5 Applying the house model to message organization.

This basic framework—using your claim or goal to identify relevant information/ evidence/backing that your co-communicators need (the unspoken warrant)— helps you achieve your goal of informing the team about your meeting. Further, this approach fits nicely (see Figure 5.5) within the basic "introduction—body— conclusion" pattern introduced earlier in this chapter.

Thus, to make a logical argument, you need to make a clear claim, support it adequately with evidence, and clearly tie your evidence to the claim. Determining which evidence will be most persuasive (team skills vs. sales numbers, for example) depends on your co-communicators. Luckily, you have carefully considered your co-communicators and planned your message accordingly.

Information and Organizing Strategy: Message Sidedness

A complementary approach to organizing the information provided in a message is message sidedness. Message sidedness helps you to determine what type of information to present to be most persuasive, so it is most applicable to persuasive goals—like the scenario in which you are trying to convince your co-communicators to increase entry-level employee salaries. Three forms of arguments[8] that incorporate different types of information can be used to structure your overall (i.e., macro) message.

	Two-sided refutational message	One-sided message	Two-sided nonrefutational message
Message	Presents arguments in favor of persuader's position, mentions counterarguments, and refutes counterarguments	Presents only arguments in favor of persuader's position	Presents arguments in favor of persuader's position and mentions counterarguments without refuting them
Effectiveness	More persuasive overall in most situations	More persuasive for co-communicators who agree with claim	Least persuasive across situations
Example	Favorable: • Company's salaries lower than those of competitors • Internally promoted employees better performers • Internally promoted employees less likely to leave Unfavorable: • Company lacks money to raise entry-level employee salaries Refutation: • Company turnover costs will decrease if salaries raised, covering difference	Favorable: • Company's salaries lower than those of competitors • Internally promoted employees better performers • Internally promoted employees less likely to leave	Favorable: • Company's salaries lower than those of competitors • Internally promoted employees better performers • Internally promoted employees less likely to leave Unfavorable: • Company lacks money to raise entry-level employee salaries

So, typically you do not want to avoid the opposing side of an argument. Your messages will generally be more persuasive if you include the opposing side as a counterclaim. Your SPACE analysis should help you understand the potential objections to your claim or any competing claims. Respond to these concerns within your own argument. Even when your audience is already favorable, this strategy might make them less likely to be swayed by weak, but unrefuted, arguments.[8] Including and refuting counterclaims allows you to find common ground with more of your co-communicators. It also makes you look more credible because you appear to be knowledgeable about the entirety of the debate rather than just being biased or uniformed. You may want to include several counterclaims to show that you have thoroughly researched the topic.

Conclusion

Developing your message is an iterative process. Depending on your medium, you will work through drafts or practice saying your message and make modifications based on what is working and what it not. Regardless of your medium, you should identify your key points, gather information to support your points through research, decide whether to be direct or indirect in your message, outline your message, structure your argument, and then revisit points in this process until your message seems appropriate.

Key Chapter Takeaways

- Identify your key points.
- Gather evidence to support your key points, considering the authority, bias, content, and currency of your sources.
- Give credit for other people's ideas in your message to strengthen you argument.
- Present the main idea right away (i.e., be direct) when your audience will agree with your message, prefers or requires directness, and/or is unlikely to feel threatened by your message.
- Present your reasoning or evidence before your main idea (i.e., be indirect) when your audience does not agree with your message and/or is likely to feel threatened by your message or when your message requires a logical argument building to your point.
- Use an outline to organize your points, supporting evidence, and message approach.
- Make claims supported by evidence (or grounds), tying this evidence to the claim through a warrant.

- Consider the type of evidence you need to present to support your overarching claim, and refute counterarguments as necessary.

- Revisit these steps as necessary in whatever order works given the nature of the communicative task. Remember, message development is part of the iterative ADE process.

Endnotes

[1] BusinessDictionary.com. (n.d.). *Iterative process*. Retrieved from http://www.businessdictionary.com/definition/iterative-process.html

[2] Montana State University (n.d.) *The ABCs of evaluating information resources.* Retrieved from http://lgdata.s3-website-us-east-1.amazonaws.com/docs/812/409021/ABCs_of_Evaluating_Information _Resources.pdf

[3] Jansen, F., & Janssen, D. (2013). Effects of directness in bad-news e-mails and voice mails. *Journal of Business Communication, 50,* 362–382. doi: 10.1177/0021943613497053

[4] Weston, A. (2009). *A rulebook for arguments* (4th ed.) Indianapolis, IN: Hackett Publishing Company, Inc.

[5] Park, H. S., Levine, T. R., Westerman, C. Y. K., Orfgen, T., & Foregger, S. (2007). The effects of argument quality and involvement type on attitude formation and attitude change: A test of dual-process and social judgment predictions. *Human Communication Research, 33,* 81–102. doi:10.1111/j.1468-2958.2007.00290.x

[6] Yukl, G., Falbe, C. M., & Youn, J. Y. (1993). Patterns of influence behavior for managers. *Group & Organization Management, 18,* 5–28.

[7] Toulmin, S. E. (2003). *The uses of argument.* Cambridge: Cambridge University Press.

[8] Allen, M. (1991). Meta-analysis comparing the persuasiveness of one-sided and two-sided messages. *Western Journal of Speech Communication, 55,* 390–404.

Chapter 6

Review of the Competent Workplace Communication Approach

The preceding chapters characterized communication competence and presented information to help you analyze situations, develop communication behaviors and skills, and evaluate your choices. This chapter aims to put all that information together in a way that will help you respond to any communication task. Because competent communicators are sophisticated in their approach to communication situations, these guidelines provide you with a framework that is meant to facilitate your thought process. Rather than providing answers or solutions that will "work every time," these guidelines serve as a reminder of what you have learned. To put everything together, this chapter will walk you through three phases in the iterative process of communication. Experiment with what works in different situations, with different co-communicators, and with different tasks. Doing so will improve your communication competence far more than treating these guidelines as a checklist! To summarize, here's how the pieces of the puzzle fit together:

Phase 1: Analyze SPACE

Phase 2: Develop Your Message

1. Identify key points

2. Research topic

3. Choose direct or indirect approach

4. Outline

5. Structure argument and messages

6. Draft/compose/rehearse

Phase 3: Evaluate Message and Communicative SPACE

Phase 1: SPACE Process for Analyzing Communication

Competent communication is Strategic, People Centered, Appropriate, Correct & Concise, and Ethical. This framework both reminds you of the considerations for analysis and provides you with a process you can follow. This section highlights considerations relevant to each characteristic of competent communication during the analyzing phase of the communication process.

S. What specific action, response, outcome, and/or resource are you trying to obtain through your communication? Is that goal primarily persuasive or informative?

Are you trying to develop, maintain, or end a relationship with your co-communicator(s)?

How do you want your co-communicator(s) to see you? How do you wish to present yourself?

P. With whom are you communicating?

What should be SAID to your co-communicators?

Situation: What are your co-communicators' goals? How do your goals relate to those of your co-communicators? How receptive will your co-communicators be to your goals? Are there any threats to your co-communicators' sense of control or self-esteem in this situation?

Attitudes: How might your co-communicators feel about the message you have to convey? Does your message threaten your co-communicators' sense of control or their self-esteem? What opinions will your co-communicators already have about the situation? How might your co-communicators respond to your message?

Information: What do your co-communicators already know? What information do you need to provide? What misinformation will you have to correct?

Demographics: What are your co-communicators like? How might that affect how you choose to communicate with them? For example, are they likely to expect a certain level of formality or to prefer a certain medium? Where are your co-communicators located? How much diversity in attitudes and information is there?

Who else might see your communication?

A. Is the message you need to send

- ambiguous/open to interpretation?
- confidential?
- requiring documentation?
- time sensitive?
- lengthy?

Given the nature of the message, your strategy, the people involved, and the organizational context, what medium would be most appropriate?

Would your strategy and co-communicators be best served by a direct or indirect approach?

C. What conventions should you follow given the medium you have chosen?

What information is vital and what could be removed?

E. What do you feel is the ethical way to approach the situation?

Phase 2: Iterative Process of Message Development

This section reminds you of the specifics of developing a message. Though for simplicity this process is presented as a series of steps, keep in mind that this process is meant to be iterative.

1. Identify key points

   • Translate your goal into a topic statement or thesis.
   • What key points need to be addressed to be effective in achieving your goals?
   • What information do your co-communicators need to know?

2. Research topic

   • What primary and secondary sources would help you make your key points?
   • Do the authority, bias, content, and currency (ABCs) of each source make it suitable to your message?
   • What information do you need to properly cite your sources?

3. Choose direct or indirect approach

   • Would your strategy and co-communicators be best served by a direct or indirect approach? Will your co-communicators:

• Agree with or be unopposed to the information/argument you present?	• Disagree with or be opposed to the information/argument you present?
• Prefer a direct approach?	• Be presented with a logical argument that builds to your recommendation, key point, or goal?
• Be likely to overlook your key points if not presented directly?	• Be likely to devote time and focus to your message?
• Feel that their self-esteem is not affected by your key points?	• Feel that their self-esteem is threatened by your key points?
• Feel that their sense of autonomy or choice is not affected by your key points?	• Feel that their sense of autonomy or choice is threatened by your key points?
Responses in this column suggest that a direct approach is appropriate.	**Responses in this column suggest that an indirect approach is appropriate.**

Evaluate your responses and make the choice that seems most appropriate given the context.

4. Outline

   • What should go in the introduction, body, and conclusion?
   • Does your outline map to the direct or indirect approach you decided to use?

      - A direct outline will present the main point right away.
      - An indirect outline will build to the main point after presenting the argument.

   • In what order should your key points be addressed to be effective in achieving your goals?

      - Present a clear preview statement as the last sentence of your introduction.

   • What content (e.g., sources) can you use to support each key point?

5. Structure argument and messages

   • Do you build a house in the overall structure of your message?
   • Do you build a house in each paragraph or section of your message?
   • Which message sidedness approach are you following (i.e., two-sided refutational or one-sided)?

6. Draft/compose/rehearse

- Do you need to revisit any aspects of this iterative process now that you have a message draft? (Psst…Moving on to Phase 3 will help you recognize opportunities for revision.)

Phase 3: Evaluating Message and Communicative SPACE

Competent communication is Strategic, People Centered, Appropriate, Correct & Concise, and Ethical. In order to achieve these goals, message need to present effective arguments. The discussion below highlights considerations relevant to each characteristic of competent communication during the evaluating phase of the communication process. These guidelines are useful to evaluate both your own communication and other's communication.

S. Can you identify the message's goals? How successful is the message in achieving those goals?

Are the key points necessary for achieving the message's goals addressed?

Does the message consistently follow the house structure at the macro and micro levels to make a strong argument?

P. How will this message be viewed by targeted and secondary co-communicators?

What is SAID?

Situation: Does the message focus on the needs of the co-communicators? Does the message recognize the goals of the co-communicators? How receptive will your co-communicators be to this message?

Attitudes: Does this message reflect an understanding of co-communicators' feelings? Does this message show an understanding of co-communicators' opinions about the situation? Does this message anticipate co-communicators' potential responses?

Information: Does this message provide all information needed by co-communicators? Does this message correct misinformation in a respectful manner?

Demographics: Does this message address the particular concerns related to co-communicator preferences, locations, and diversity?

A. Given the nature of the message, strategy, and the people involved, does the message seem appropriate in terms of the medium used?

Given the nature of the message, strategy, and the people involved, does the message seem appropriate in terms of the information provided?

Do the ABCs of the primary and secondary sources make them appropriate for inclusion?

Does the message have a clear introduction, body, and conclusion with appropriate information included in each one given the approach taken?

Given the nature of the message, strategy, and the people involved, does the message seem appropriate in terms of the message strategies (i.e., direct vs. indirect approach, message sidedness) used?

C. Is the message correct?

Is the formatting correct based on the conventions of the medium used?

What information is vital and what could be removed?

Is the information presented concisely?

Are sources cited correctly?

Are there any grammatical, word choice, or language errors?

E. Do you feel this is the right way to approach the situation?

If this message were disseminated to a much wider (even nonbusiness audience), how would they view it?

If you have been evaluating your own message, you might need to return to the analysis or development phases to make improvements. If you are evaluating a co-communicator's message, your evaluation will affect your perceptions of that person and your response to the message.

Reflecting to Improve Communication Competency

After interacting with your co-communicators and learning their reactions to your message, remember that the ADE process is cyclical. Reflect on your message. Was this competent communication? Both your own evaluation and the feedback you receive need to be taken into consideration as you approach future communication tasks. Competent communicators use their experiences—successes and failures—to continue to improve their communication skills. These guidelines are meant to help communication constitute effective interactions, relationships, and organizations.

SPACE Model for Competent Communication

	Strategic	People-Focused	Appropriate	Correct & Concise	Ethical
Concept	Focused on goals	Concerned with co-communicators and their perspective	Uses acceptable medium to present professional message in logical manner	Follows standards to present succinct, focused message	Takes implications of message for all co-communicators into account
Considerations for Planning	What specific action, response, outcome, and/ or resource are you trying to obtain through your communication? Is that goal primarily persuasive or informative? Are you trying to develop, maintain, or end a relationship with your co-communicator(s)? How do you want your co-communicator(s) to see you? How do you wish to present yourself?	With whom are you communicating? What should be SAID to your co-communicator(s)? Who else might see your communication?	Is the message you need to send: ambiguous/open to interpretation, confidential, requiring documentation, time sensitive, or lengthy? Given the nature of the message, your strategy, the people involved, and the organizational context, what medium would be most appropriate? Would your strategy and co-communicators be best served by a direct or indirect approach?	What conventions should you follow given the medium you have chosen? What information is vital and what could be removed?	What do you feel is the ethical way to approach the situation?
Considerations for Evaluating	Can you identify the message's goals? How successful is the message in achieving those goals? Are the key points needed to be effective in achieving the message's goals addressed? Does the message consistently follow the house structure at the macro and micro levels to make a strong argument?	How will this message be viewed by targeted and secondary co-communicators? What is SAID?	Given the nature of the message, strategy, and the people involved, does the message seem appropriate in terms of the medium used and the information provided? Do the ABCs of the primary and secondary sources make them appropriate for inclusion? Does the message have a clear introduction, body, and conclusion with appropriate information included in each one given the approach taken? Given the nature of the message, strategy, and the people involved, does the message seem appropriate in terms of the message strategies (i.e., direct vs. indirect approach, message sidedness) used?	Is the message correct? Is the formatting correct based on the conventions of the medium used? What information is vital and what could be removed? Is the information presented concisely? Are sources cited correctly? Are there any grammatical, word choice, or language errors?	Do you feel this is the right way to approach the situation? If this message were disseminated to a much wider (even non-business audience), how would they view it?

Part 4

Developing Your Skill Repertoire

Adapted image © VLADGRIN, 2014. Used under license from Shutterstock, Inc.

Chapter
7

Communication Competence in Oral Media

Adapted image © VLADGRIN, 2014.
Used under license from Shutterstock, Inc.

When to Use Oral Media

Phone calls, presentations, group meetings, video conferences, and face-to-face conversations are the forms of oral media introduced in Chapter 4. Compared to electronic media or traditional written media, these forms of oral media are most appropriate in certain contexts, namely, when

- the message requires rich cues
- immediate feedback is desirable
- no permanent record is needed

- interaction can be synchronous
- the message can be delivered without need to edit

These general guidelines apply to all forms of oral media. Of course, different forms of oral media also offer different strengths and should be used in different contexts.

Ideal SPACE				
Phone calls	Presentations	Group meetings	Video conferences	Face-to-Face conversations
Few co-communicators	Co-communicators need information delivery, less discussion	Small group of co-communicators who need to actively participate	Small group of co-communicators with access to necessary technology	Confidential messages
Co-communicator(s) available at same time, but not necessarily in the same place	Co-communicator(s) available at the same time and same place	Co-communicator(s) available at the same time and place	Co-communicator(s) available at the same time but not in the same place	Co-communicator(s) available at the same time and place
Ambiguous messages that might require real-time modifications				Ambiguous messages that might require real-time modifications
Confidential, time-sensitive messages				

Encoding/Decoding Skills of Special Interest

These forms of oral media require diverse encoding and decoding skills—mainly because they offer richer cues than most traditional and electronic media. Using the encoding/decoding framework discussed in Chapter 2, we will explore how competent communicators can use and attend to these cues.

Language Use and Clear Verbal Expression

Oral media lack "redo" capability because they are synchronous. You cannot go through multiple drafts until you get something exactly right as you can with other forms of media. However, communication competence is still evaluated, in part, based on how correct and concise you are. Planning and practice are particularly important but are often considered only for formal presentations. While practice is especially vital for presentations, which require you to carry a very heavy load in the interaction, practicing (meaning saying out loud) other forms of oral communication can also be helpful. Following the process for structuring your message from Chapter 5 will help. At the very least, an outline can be helpful to keep conversations, meetings, and presentations on topic and on time.

Appropriate Nonverbal Communication

One often misquoted statistic about the importance of nonverbal cues actually provides insight into our inherent beliefs about these cues. You may have heard that research shows that over 90% of meaning comes from nonverbal cues. The book *Silent Messages*[1] summarized previous research on the role of nonverbal cues when people provide inconsistent messages (meaning that verbal and nonverbal messages conflict) about their attitudes and feelings. In these specific situations, 55% of a speaker's message is conveyed through body language, 38% is tone of voice, and only 7% are the actual words spoken. Thus, 93% of meaning came from nonverbal cues when verbal and nonverbal messages about feelings and attitudes conflicted. Though this finding has been inaccurately shorthanded as 93% of meaning comes from nonverbal cues, the fact that few question this shorthand speaks to the weight we put on nonverbal cues in interactions.[2] Because we send so many different types of nonverbal cues—particularly in face-to-face interactions—understanding that our co-communicators are attending to those cues and weighing them heavily in their efforts to reach shared meaning is valuable information.

Often, people think about nonverbal cues as what we do with our bodies. However, we typically attend to an array of nonverbal cues in our interactions with others. Beyond just tone and formatting, these forms of media offer vocal cues and most offer kinesics, which makes these forms of media "richer" (in Chapter 4 terms) than traditional written and electronic messages. Here is a summary[3] of the cues nonverbal researchers study, all of which are applicable for face-to-face conversations and, to a certain extent, other oral media:

- Kinesics (body communication)
  - Facial expressions
  - Eyes and eye contact
  - Gestures
  - Touch
- Physical characteristics/Appearance
- Proxemics (use of space)[4]
  - Intimate distance (0–18 inches): Typically inappropriate in work settings
  - Personal distance (18 inches–4 feet): Reserved for handshakes and interpersonal conversations with close colleagues
  - Social distance (4–10 feet): Typically preferred for professional discussions
  - Public distance (over 10 feet): Preferred for public presentations
- Paravocalics (vocal style and tone)[5]
  - Pitch
  - Volume
  - Timbre (quality)
  - Resonance (pronunciation)
  - Speech rate
  - Use of fillers and/or pauses
  - Stress or emphasis
- Chronemics (use of time)
- Aesthetics (physical space or environment)

Controlling all these nonverbal cues would be incredibly challenging. Often, we attend to only a few as we communicate. However, because interpretation of cues is largely automatic and unconscious, our co-communicators will seek out messages sent by our nonverbal cues and will attempt to interpret them.

You can consciously use this to your advantage. One consistent research finding is that subtle mirroring of co-communicators' nonverbal behaviors leads to positive rapport. People actually engage in this behavior fairly naturally by accommodating their paravocalics to converge with (or match those) of others.[6] You can take this further by using certain nonverbal cues to have other people view you positively. In many situations, smiling, direct body orientation that involves leaning toward the other person slightly, open body posture, moderate eye contact, and appropriate touch will build liking and rapport.[7] As you know at this point, competent communication is somewhat situationally dependent, and nonverbal cues are no exception. Whether a specific cue is viewed as appropriate (or inappropriate) depends on the context. For example, if you are sharing news of a promotion with an employee, a smile would be an appropriate facial expression. Conversely, if you are firing an employee, a smile would be inappropriate.

Being consistent in your nonverbal cues is key. Though verbal messages tend to be processed word by word and line by line, nonverbal cues are often interpreted as a whole.[8] In other words, do all of your nonverbal cues send a message that you are interested? Or, are you sending inconsistent cues, such as facing a person with open body posture but breaking off eye contact to look at your phone or around the room? Your co-communicators will (largely unconsciously) attend to the cues you provide and interpret them together.

Nonverbal cues are tied to the situation in which they are expressed and also to the verbal or language cues used.[9] Your co-communicators will take in the gestalt of your nonverbal cues and compare them with your verbal cues. Verbal and nonverbal cues can interact in different ways.[10] The relationship of nonverbal communication with verbal communication may be as follows:

- Reinforcing
  - Nonverbal message matches verbal message
  - Example: Nodding head while saying yes
- Complementing/Accenting
  - Nonverbal message stresses verbal message
  - Example: Vocal stress and body language convey excitement while saying yes
- Substituting
  - Nonverbal message replaces the verbal message
  - Example: Nodding instead of saying yes

- Conflicting
  - Verbal and nonverbal messages are in contrast
  - Example: Shaking head while saying yes

Even if we do not intend to send a particular message, our co-communicators may understand our nonverbal cues in unintended ways. Understanding that these interpretations can interfere with our ability to reach shared meanings will help you to be a more competent communicator. You cannot control all of your cues, but you can recognize the power of those cues and seek to understand how your verbal and nonverbal messages are interpreted by your co-communicators.

Cultural Awareness

Nonverbal cues are culturally dependent. Though evidence[11] supports comparability in facial expressions across cultures, the appropriateness of expressing emotions through facial expressions still differs across cultures. All information presented in this text is based on research conducted on mainstream U.S. culture. Co-communicators from different cultures (or U.S. subcultures) may have different norms for cues such as eye contact or proxemics. Competent communicators do not necessarily need to memorize the nonverbal norms of other cultures. Instead, they are aware that differences may exist and are cognizant of how their own nonverbal behaviors may be interpreted in unintended ways when communicating cross-culturally. When evaluating the messages of their co-communicators in cross-cultural situations, competent communicators carefully consider nonverbal behaviors.

Attention

Because these media are synchronous, attention is especially relevant. Unlike with a written document (e.g., a report or an email), you cannot "re-read" a conversation. Whether on the phone, participating in a meeting, or talking face-to-face, you need to be present and focused on the message. Of course, clarifying questions are acceptable (and demonstrate listening if done correctly—see below). However, asking someone to repeat something because you were not paying attention will not be viewed as competent. Do not attempt to multitask or use other forms of media during the interaction. Focus your attention on your co-communicators to take advantage of the strengths of these forms of media.

Active Listening, Interpretation, and the Ability to Respond Appropriately

We spend roughly half of our work day listening. Listening is "how individuals perceive, interpret, evaluate, and respond to messages."[12] Listening is a vital—but too often ignored—part of being a competent communicator. When one study asked participants to describe communicatively competent co-workers, they used many listening-related attributes such as "listens well" and "is open-minded." Thus, being a competent communicator includes being a competent listener.[13] Good listeners are rated as more liked, more attractive, and more trustworthy than less skilled listeners. Beyond positive interpersonal outcomes, good listeners tend to be high academic achievers and are more likely to get promoted at work.[14]

Though listening is discussed separately for simplicity here, listening and speaking are not separate tasks—neurologically speaking.[15] Our ability to listen is inextricably linked to our ability to speak. This interrelation is better reflected in current constitutive or transactional models of communication. The false dichotomy between speaking and listening comes from antiquated transmission (sender-receiver) models. Current research on and conceptualizations of listening emphasize its complexity and role in communication. One prominent communication

Special Considerations for Phone Calls

When on the phone, co-communicators have access not only to the words used to express ideas but also to the tone and vocal cues used. Because fewer nonverbal cues are available, co-communicators may be distracted by tone and vocal cues like pauses. Of course, the fact that co-communicators cannot see one another offers advantages as well. For example, co-communicators can use notes or outlines to make sure that important points are covered. However, unlike traditional written media, messages can be modified in the moment based on co-communicator reactions. Thus, phone calls offer an interesting opportunity to utilize prepared contingencies—an opportunity of which many telemarketers (for example) have been trained to take advantage.

researcher characterizes listening as a complex interplay of "(a) cognitive processes, such as attending to, understanding, receiving, and interpreting content and relational messages; (b) affective processes, such as being motivated to attend to those messages; and (c) behavioral processes, such as responding with verbal and nonverbal feedback (e.g., backchanneling, paraphrasing)."[16]

You probably will not be surprised to hear that good listeners are attentive and responsive; most popular notions of listening have provided that information. However, these attributes of good listeners do not necessarily tell you how to be a good listener. Only recently have researchers begun to measure the behaviors of good listeners. Emerging evidence suggests that those who are viewed by their co-communicators as good listeners show certain verbal and nonverbal behaviors.

After reading about nonverbal cues, you might now be surprised to learn that verbal behaviors are perceived as more indicative of good listening than nonverbal behaviors.[17] However, if you recall that listening is an inseparable aspect of the process of cocreating meaning (i.e., communicating), you will notice that these verbal behaviors aid in that process. Perhaps it is not surprising that when asked to evaluate listening skills, we intuitively recognize that many of these nonverbal behaviors can be enacted even when we are not truly listening. The verbal behaviors of good listeners summarized in the table would be harder to fake!

Behaviors of good listeners.	
Nonverbal behaviors of good listeners	**Verbal behaviors of good listeners**
• Maintain eye contact	• Provide on-topic responses
• Make appropriate facial expressions	• Elaborate on topics being discussed
• Use hand gestures	• Ask questions
• Demonstrate composure (e.g., no fidgeting)	• Offer advice, opinions, perspectives, and personal experience
	• Answer questions
	• Do not interrupt or change subject

Note: This table summarizes the findings of Bodie, St. Cyr, Pence, Rold, and Honeycutt, 2012.

Special Considerations for Video Conferences

- Test the technology before the scheduled start time.
- Prepare a contingency plan in case of technical difficulties.
  - Know how to contact attendees.
  - Have contact information for technical support.
- Connect in a quiet place with a good high-speed connection.
- Dress and sit professionally.
- Consider the background.
- Check the camera angle prior to connecting.
  - Angled down tends to be the most flattering perspective.
  - Professionalism in appearance and surroundings can be evaluated.
- Work to involve all co-communicators.
- As with all other forms of communication, attend to the conversation; don't be tempted to do other things.

Special Considerations for Presentations

When presenting to an audience, you are less likely to have the level of interaction that you get in a discussion. Thus, both you and your co-communicators (who are relatively passive) tend to focus even more strongly on your verbal and nonverbal cues than with another form of oral communication. Because we have focused on things that will generally be evaluated as competent communication across contexts, what makes for competent public speaking does not dramatically differ from what makes for competent communication generally. However, attending to some specific nonverbal and verbal aspects will improve your presentation skills. Previously, we touched on specific nonverbal cues. In presentation situations, certain nonverbal behaviors are more likely to be associated with competent communication.

- Kinesics (body communication)
  - Maintain eye contact with the audience.
  - Use gestures appropriate to the space and the context to emphasize key points.

- Physical characteristics/appearance
  - Dress professionally or at least one level above your audience.
  - Avoid distracting clothing or accessories.
  - Construct professional visual aids to enhance (rather than detract from) your appearance.

- Proxemics (use of space)
  - Recognize that Hall's rules[4] for space apply.
    · Presenters addressing large audiences should maintain 10+ feet distance when presenting.
    · Presenters addressing smaller groups or teams might be in a 4–10 feet range.
  - Move around (maintaining appropriate distance) when possible.

- Paravocalics
  - Be careful in your pronunciation and enunciation because what you say is the primary source of information for your co-communicators.
  - Avoid fillers and/or pauses.
  - Use your pitch and volume to make sure everyone can hear you.
  - Speak at a moderate rate. (Recording yourself will help you get a sense for your rate, though we often speed up when nervous.)
  - Use stress or emphasis to highlight key points.

- Chronemics
  - Stay within your allotted presentation time.
  - Do not forget to allow time for questions and/or discussion.

The organization of your speech is particularly important because your co-communicators cannot go back and revisit something they did not understand. The content of your speech will ideally cover 2–4 key points or claims. The basic format

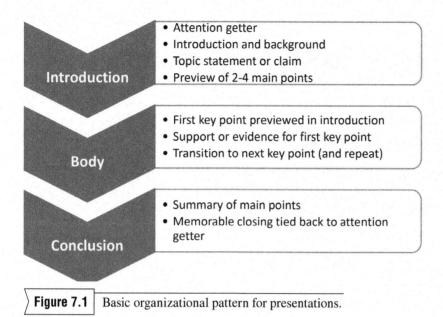

Figure 7.1 | Basic organizational pattern for presentations.

introduced in Chapter 5 for organizing your message also applies to presentations (see Figure 7.1). Some particular elements are stressed in oral presentations.

Most of the time, an outline (rather than a script) is the ideal level of structure. You should have your key points and all aspects of your argument (claim, evidence, and warrant) mapped out in your outline. If you choose to use a program like PowerPoint or Prezi as a visual aid for your presentation, this outline also serves as a basis for the slides you create. Translate major headings (i.e., those 2–4 key points or claims) into slide titles. Then, focus on the major concepts from your outline to fill in the points you would like to make. To keep slides readable and to avoid being text heavy, stick to the 6 × 6 rule for slides: no more than six bullet points with up to six words per bullet (see Figure 7.2). Use visuals in place of words when possible (such as illustrations, charts, or graphs) so that your co-communicators receive the information in more than one form. Remember, you are the focal point and the key provider of information (whether you like it or not); your visual aids are meant to support—not detract from—your verbal content.

Tips for Formatting PowerPoint Slides

- Follow the 6-x-6 rule
- Demonstrate parallelism in bullet points
- Choose appropriate design template and fonts
- Create graphics for visual concepts
- Avoid distracting format choices
- Use text concisely

> **Figure 7.2** | Formatting tips for PowerPoint.

Finally, though outlining, visual aid development, and other forms of preparation are essential to giving a good presentation, you cannot neglect practice. You need not only to think about what you will say but also to practice saying it. Because you will be presenting in front of others, practicing in front of others is ideal. Speakers stumble between their main points if they do not practice smooth transitions and may become flustered in front of an audience without practice. Consider that "The Great Communicator," former President Reagan, spent three hours a day for a week practicing his State of the Union addresses, culminating in one full day spent recording himself speaking, reviewing the recordings, and then doing it all over again.[17] His State of the Union addresses averaged 40 minutes,[18] which means that he practiced each speech approximately 38 times longer than he spent giving it to a national audience. Don't forget that because of teleprompters he could read the whole thing directly. He was not necessarily a natural-born "Great Communicator;" he consistently committed himself to becoming one. Practice might not make perfect, but it certainly makes success more likely!

For Oral Communication, Practice Makes . . . Prepared

Social Facilitation Theory[19] provides an explanation for why practice typically leads to better public speaking performance. According to this theory, the presence of others leads to a state of arousal that we label as nerves (or maybe excitement). When people are in this state, we tend to be more likely to demonstrate a habitual response. If we are well-practiced at a certain task—such as presenting our message orally—we will actually perform better in front of an audience. This is social facilitation; we have a tendency to perform better on well-practiced tasks when others are watching us compared to when we are alone. This effect is even more likely in situations in which we do not know our co-communicators well. Conversely, if we are not well prepared in such a situation, we tend to perform much worse in front of others than we would by ourselves. So, practice serves a purpose. When we communicate in the presence of others (as we do with many oral media that offer high levels of immediacy), we are likely to get nervous and/or excited. If we have practiced, those feelings will lead us to do an even better job; if we have not practiced, those feelings will lead us to do a worse job. So, nerves actually help our performance if we have practiced.

Key Chapter Takeaways

- The availability of a large number of nonverbal cues makes oral media "richer."

- In general, naturally matching your co-communicator's paravocalics, smiling, facing and leaning slightly toward your co-communicator with open body posture, and making moderate eye contact will be positively interpreted.

- Nonverbal cues and verbal cues can relate to one another in many ways. Your co-communicators will evaluate their consistency.

- The meaning of nonverbal cues is culturally determined.

- "Good listening" involves both verbal and nonverbal behaviors.

- Verbal behaviors—like asking questions and providing topical responses—are seen as better indicators of "good listening" than nonverbal behaviors like eye contact.

- Presentations put a large burden on the speaker to prepare the verbal message carefully while also attending to nonverbals when presenting.

- Practicing (ideally in front of others) is the best way to ensure successful oral communication. You only get one chance to communicate your message with oral media.

Endnotes

[1] Mehrabian, A. (1981). *Silent messages: Implicit communication of emotions and attitudes*. Belmont, CA: Wadsworth.

[2] Mehrabian, A. (2011). *"Silent messages": A wealth of information about nonverbal communication (body language)*. Retrieved from http://www.kaaj.com/psych/smorder.html

[3] Richmond, V. P., McCroskey, J. C., & Hickson, M. L. (2011). *Nonverbal behavior in interpersonal relations* (7th ed.). Boston: Allyn & Bacon.

[4] Hall, E. T. (1990). *The hidden dimension*. New York: Anchor Books.

[5] Frank, M. G., Maroulis, A., & Griffin, D. J. (2012). The voice. In D. Matsumoto, M. G. Frank, & H. S. Hwang (Eds.), *Nonverbal communication: Science and applications* (pp. 53–74). Los Angeles, CA: Sage.

[6] Giles, H., Mulac, A., Bradac, J., & Johnson, P. (1987). Speech Accommodation Theory: The first decade and beyond. In M. L. McLaughlin (Ed.), *Communication yearbook 10* (pp. 13–48). Newbury Park, CA: Sage.

[7] Matsumoto, M. G., & Hwang, H. S. (2012). Body and gestures. In D. Matsumoto, M. G. Frank, & H. S. Hwang (Eds.), *Nonverbal communication: Science and applications* (pp. 75–96). Los Angeles, CA: Sage.

[8] Andersen, P. A. (1999). *Nonverbal communication: Forms and functions*. Mountain View, CA: Mayfield.

[9] Kudesia, R.S., & Elgenbein, H.A. (2013). Nonverbal communication in the workplace. In J. A. Hall & M. L. Knapp (Eds.) *Nonverbal communication* (pp. 805–831). Berlin, Germany: de Gruyter.

[10] Ekman, P., & Friesen, W. V. (1969). The repertoire of nonverbal behavior: Categories, origins, usage, and coding. *Semiotica, 1*, 49–98. Retrieved from http://boccignone.di.unimi.it/CompAff2011_files/EkmanFriesenSemiotica.pdf

[11] Matsumoto, M. G., & Hwang, H. S. (2012). Body and gestures. In D. Matsumoto, M. G. Frank, & H. S. Hwang (Eds.), *Nonverbal communication: Science and applications* (pp. 75–96). Los Angeles, CA: Sage.

[12] Kirtley, M.D., & Honeycutt, J. M. (1996). Listening styles and their correspondence with second guessing. *Communication Research Reports, 13*, 174–182.

[13] Haas, J. W., & Arnold, C. L. (1995). An examination of the role of listening in judgments of communication competence in co-workers. *The Journal of Business Communication, 32*, 123–139.

[14] Neglia, A. (2013, September 6). The #1 skill of extremely likable (and successful) people. Retrieved from http://www.grandparents.com/health-and-wellbeing/emotional-wellbeing/attention-span

[15] Berger, C. R. (2011). Listening is for acting. *International Journal of Listening, 25*, 104–110. doi: 10.1080/10904018.2011.536477

[16] Bodie, G. D. (2013). Issues in the measurement of listening. *Communication Research Reports, 30*, 76–84. doi: 10.1080/08824096.2012.733981

[17] Bodie , G.D., St. Cyr, K., Pence, M., Rold, M., & Honeycutt, J. (2012). Listening competence in initial interactions I: Distinguishing between what listening is and what listeners do. *International Journal of Listening, 26*, 1–28. doi: 10.1080/10904018.2012.639645

[18] Walker, T. J. (n.d.) *Public speaking training*. Retrieved from http://www.howcast.com/guides/931-Public-Speaking-Training

[19] The American Presidency Project. (2014). *Length of State of the Union messages and addresses (in minutes)*. Retrieved from http://www.presidency.ucsb.edu/sou_minutes.php

[20] Zajonc, R. B. (1965). Social facilitation. *Science, 149*, 269–274. Retrieved from http://www2.psych.ubc.ca/~schaller/Psyc591Readings/Zajonc1965.pdf

Adapted image © VLADGRIN, 2014.
Used under license from Shutterstock, Inc.

Chapter 8

Communication Competence in Electronic Media

When to Use Electronic Media

Electronic messages (here limited to email, text messages, websites, and social media) are best when you need to distribute simple information quickly to a geographically dispersed group of co-communicators. Though I rarely use the word "never," I will use it here. Never use electronic messages to deliver sensitive or confidential information! Because these messages go out quickly and cannot be "taken back," never use them to communicate anything you would not want shared with a wider set of co-communicators. Compared to oral media or traditional written media, these forms of electronic media are most appropriate in certain contexts, namely, when

- the message needs to be delivered quickly
- privacy is not required
- the level of detail needed is low
- feedback is desired, but immediacy is less important

These general guidelines apply to all forms of electronic media. Of course, different forms of electronic media also offer different strengths and should be used in different contexts.

Ideal SPACE			
Email	**Text Messages**	**Websites**	**Social Media**
Quickly disperses messages to any number of co-communicators in any location	Informal, extremely short messages	Message does not require personalization to specific co-communicators	Content creation from co-communicators desired
Attachments might be used to share longer messages	Relatively quick response desired	Nonconfidential information (for public websites)	Widespread access to information desired
Relatively straightforward messages that convey routine, nonconfidential information	Straightforward messages that convey routine, nonconfidential information	Widespread access to information desired	Non-confidential information
Drafting preferable to real-time modifications to message		Multimedia content	Real-time clarifications might be necessary
		Interaction with co-communicators less important	
		Drafting preferable to real-time modifications to message	

Think before Hitting "Send"

One of the strengths of electronic media—the ability to reply quickly to dispersed co-communicators—can be a double-edged sword. Just because you can reply instantly does not mean that you should. Remember that with fewer cues some messages can be misinterpreted. Though email programs like Outlook offer a "Recall This Message" option, this option often does not prevent your message from being read for various reasons. So, approach email and all forms of electronic communication with the knowledge that once you hit "send," your message is out there. You cannot take back messages that go out—even if they are unprofessional, emotional, or incomplete. Because completely removing an electronic message is practically impossible, exercising caution is key.

How can you work to avoid mistakenly sending an electronic message?

- Carefully look at the distribution list/receivers of the message. Make sure only your targeted co-communicators are included. Avoid hitting "Reply All" on a message targeted toward a smaller group or individual.

- Draft offline. If you are preparing an important message or feeling emotional when composing a message, consider composing it offline (i.e., not in the program in which you plan to send it). For example, using a word processing program will allow you to save the message and make revisions until you feel it is ready. You can then paste directly into the program you wish to use in sending the message.

- Consider who else might see your message. Postings to social media can be seen by broad audiences unintentionally. Emails and text messages can be forwarded (purposefully or accidently).

Encoding/Decoding Skills of Special Interest

Using the encoding/decoding framework discussed in Chapter 2, we will explore how competent communicators can use and attend to these cues.

Language Use and Clear Verbal Expression

In some ways, text messages and social media have given rise to whole new forms of language. Acronyms and hashtags allow us to take advantage of these particular platforms. Acronyms allow us to convey frequently used phrases quickly, without need to type them out. Hashtags allow us to connect our ideas on a particular topic to those of other social media users. Of course, both acronyms and hashtags have a use. However, in workplace communication, competence might mean using them differently. In business interactions, avoid using acronyms or other abbreviations in most texts—unless you are absolutely certain your co-communicator(s) will understand them. When you think of it, many texting acronyms do not convey professional or necessary messages (e.g., omg or ttyl). Because hashtags can help you to maximize the benefits of social media, distill hashtags down to important themes that will allow for connection with other users—not as a #jumbledwaytoexpressyourself. Maximize the benefits of these forms of media through the language you use, and carefully gear that language toward your professional environment.

Grammatical conventions and rules are particularly contested in forms of electronic media. You might ask, "Why do I need to use proper grammar when I text or post to social media? Most people don't." Of course, the answer is because you understand what competent communication looks like and how such mistakes can affect our goals (particularly self-presentation goals) and our aims for shared meaning. The "correct and concise" standard for competent communication is particularly pertinent for electronic media. Because verbal cues (your words) are central, grammatical conventions—like capitalization and punctuation—help make those cues more understandable. Further, your co-communicators will not be able to turn off the part of their brain that raises red flags for spelling or grammatical errors just because they are reading a text message. Remember that smart phones and computers are useful tools, but you are smarter! Spellcheck and autocorrect can be friends or foes; read your professional messages and postings before you send or post them.

Conciseness is also particularly important for electronic communication—especially emails and text messages. Your co-communicators will expect these messages to be relatively brief compared to a memo or report, with text messaging being reserved for the shortest messages. A good rule of thumb is to limit your electronic messages to one screen. In other words, your co-communicators should not have to scroll to read your complete message. A text message is, thus, considerably shorter than email because a smart phone screen is smaller than a computer screen.

Keep in mind that even when you are using forms of electronic media your co-communicators are likely to use the same standards to evaluate your messages. Is your message clear? Do you provide the content necessary to understand meaning? Is your message organized logically? Show care for the words you choose, correctly presenting those words and conveying the appropriate tone in your electronic messages.

Appropriate Nonverbal Communication

Text and email messages are particularly "lean" forms of media (see the chart in Chapter 4)—meaning they offer few cues. Nonverbal cues are even more limited than verbal ones. However, do not assume that these forms of media eliminate nonverbal cues completely.[1] From the extensive list of nonverbal cues we have been using, three are pertinent to electronic media (though not to all forms of electronic media).

- Kinesics: Facial expressions are not an available cue in most forms of electronic media. Because we largely cannot "see" our co-communicators in electronic media interactions, straightforward messages are best conveyed. For example, humor and sarcasm are unlikely to translate well because we lack the nonverbal cues (like a wink) to let co-communicators in on the joke. Because electronic media are so lean, certain textual cues have arisen to help convey emotion that we might typically glean from facial expressions—namely, emoticons. Though emoticons are useful substitutes for facial expressions in nonprofessional communication, a smiley face in an email to a client will likely not be seen as professional. Sticking to the types of messages best conveyed through email will prevent you from relying on emoticons.

- Paravocalics: Often, the way words are said gives us insight into our co-communicators' meaning. Again, humor and sarcasm are difficult to detect in electronic media interactions because we lack vocal cues—like tone of voice. Your co-communicators will look to textual cues to provide the information that they normally get through tone. As discussed above, proper punctuation and capitalization increase the likelihood of coming to a shared understanding of content. They also prevent co-communicators from interpreting emotion based on the appearance of our text. For example, use of CAPS will be interpreted as volume—namely, yelling. Use of *italics*, <u>underlining</u>, or **bold** font will be interpreted as stress or emphasis. Being cognizant of the fact that your co-communicators will interpret formatting as meaning cues should inform the way you present your message.

- Chronemics: Your co-communicators might attend to the rate of interaction. Though these forms of media are not necessarily synchronous, there is an expectation of fairly prompt response to emails, text messages, or social media posts. Your co-communicators will attempt to make sense of delayed responses—even if they are simply caused by a dead cell phone battery.

- Aesthetics: Crafting your own websites or creating a personal page on some forms of social media allows you to create an aesthetic environment that can contribute to the verbal content you include on the site. However, most forms of electronic media do not allow for many aesthetic cues.

Interpretation and the Ability to Respond Appropriately

Forms of electronic media can be tempting when you are engaged in other channels/forms of communication. Have you ever browsed a social network or sent a text when engaged in a face-to-face form of communication? The prevalence of electronic media in our daily lives leads many of us to multitask—particularly to attempt to communicate using more than one medium simultaneously. Have you ever been talking with someone while reading or composing something and accidently said a word from the message you are writing that does not fit into your conversation? Such incidents are unavoidable, given that research strongly suggests we are not capable of simultaneously attending to two separate communicative tasks.

With the rise of electronic forms of communication, more of us are attempting to "multitask" by engaging in multiple communicative tasks at once. In reality, we unconsciously switch between tasks, rather than completing two tasks simultaneously. As a result, we lose information as we shift from the "rules" for listening to the "rules" for texting. Our brains must first identify the new task and then access the "rules" for performing that task before we can actually shift to focusing on a second task. This "rule activation" takes several tenths of a second.[2] That might not sound like much, but it adds up when we repeatedly switch back and forth between tasks (i.e., multitask). Thus, multitasking may seem more efficient on the surface but may actually take more time in the end.

In addition to not saving time, we are also not completing communicative tasks at the same cognitive level if we are attempting to "multitask" our communication. By studying the brains of people attempting to complete multiple tasks at once, researchers have found that our brains cope with additional tasks by shifting responsibility from the part of the brain that stores and recalls information to the part of the brain that takes care of rote, repetitive activities. When multitasking, we might complete activities, but we don't recall specifics. Higher levels of the brain related to memory and learning are not activated. Our brains focus on task completion rather than the content of the task itself.[3] Mindless tasks might be acceptable to complete simultaneous with other activities, but hopefully by this point in the book we have established that most communicative tasks are not mindless and likely require access to the storage and recall areas of the brain.

Unfortunately, multitasking is becoming increasingly commonplace. Among college students:

- 53% report consuming some other form of media while watching television
- 58% multitask while reading
- 62% multitask while using the computer
- 63% multitask while listening to music[4]

So, even given the obvious difficulties in our attempts to multitask, why do we still attempt to engage in multiple communication tasks at once? The same theory we used to identify what type of media will be appropriate in Chapter 4 provides some explanation of when and why we might do so. We are more likely to engage in this form of multitasking when others do so and when we perceive that it is okay.[5] For example, if we are in a meeting and see our colleagues checking their smartphones, we are more likely to do so. Of course, this means that choosing not to engage in this form of multitasking will have a comparable effect. If we refrain from this form of multitasking and make clear to others that we do not see this behavior as appropriate, we are likely to be successful in discouraging it—at least in specific situations.

Special Considerations for Social Media

Social networks—such as Facebook, Twitter, and LinkedIn—are increasingly useful forms of electronic media for professionals and businesses alike. Individual professionals use social networks to connect with colleagues and clients, exchange ideas, find jobs, and highlight their professional strengths and accomplishments. Businesses connect with customers and employees, share company news, and exchange ideas. Social media are distinct from traditional websites in one key way. Traditional websites were simply "consumed" by users; social media sites are simultaneously created and consumed by users—creating more of a bottom-up experience than a top-down one.[6]

Of course, with these opportunities come potential risks for organizations and professionals. Like other forms of electronic media, social media messages can be widely dispersed almost immediately. This immediacy is both a benefit and a risk of social networks. Companies, for example, can immediately respond to customer concerns or inquiries. However, failure to respond appropriately or in a timely manner can hurt a company. Individual users also face similar tradeoffs. Job candidates have access to multiple job opportunities across the county and the world, and those companies often have access to job candidates' social media information. Nearly 70% of businesses have rejected a job candidate due to social media blunders such as inappropriate posts or poor communication. The same number of businesses report hiring a job candidate due to his/her social media presence, especially when they seem professional and creative and demonstrate good communication skills on social media.[7] Social media offer risks and benefits to organizations and individuals alike.

If you do a simple search online, you will find a plethora of tips for communication success on social media. Essentially, the tips for success mirror the guidelines for competent communication presented here: know your goals and your co-communicators, craft appropriate messages using the best media for your goals and co-communicators, be concise and correct, and be ethical. For example, *Entrepreneur* magazine's "tips to power up your social media" include knowing your customers and crediting your sources.[8] Providing specific tips on how to be successful on a (likely soon to be outdated) social media platform is not the goal here. The idea is that competent communication looks largely the same—regardless of the media—because it takes into account which medium is most appropriate given the context. Social media work best in certain situations, and the "rules" for success are pretty general (as in any situation). Because you are a competent communicator who is aware of the strengths and weaknesses (and, therefore, appropriateness) of certain forms of media, you will carefully consider your communication in any situation—regardless of the medium in which you are communicating.

Of course, careful consideration doesn't mean taking a week to respond to a post on social media. Social media platforms require frequent interaction with co-communicators. Social media should be used to interconnect businesses, employees, and customers for frequent positive interactions.[9] Taking advantage of the nature of social media—where everyone can contribute—is a key benefit (and risk) of this medium.

Social Media and You

- Think before you post.
- Don't share sensitive or inappropriate information or photos.
- Be careful when blocking colleagues or turning down friend invitations.
- Keep your profile professional.
- Use different social media platforms to maximize unique benefits and networks.
- Highlight awards, professional goals, and accomplishments.

Special Considerations for Email

Because email is a major form of communication in organizations today, your co-communicators will especially appreciate concise, correct communication. On average, corporate email users send and receive around 120 email messages per day.[10] This number is expected to stay relatively steady, despite the additional media (e.g., social networks and text messaging) increasingly used for corporate communication. This volume of email takes up around 30% of the average knowledge worker's time.[11]

Emails are, in some ways, now taking on the predominant role that traditional written messages such as letters and memos played in organizations in the past. Though letters and memos are still utilized in organizations, they

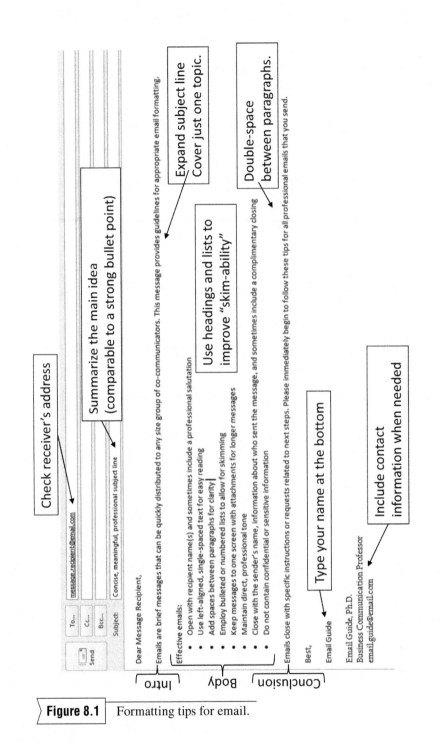

Figure 8.1 Formatting tips for email.

The figure shows an email formatting example with the following annotations:

- Check receiver's address
- Summarize the main idea (comparable to a strong bullet point)
- Expand subject line
- Cover just one topic.
- Double-space between paragraphs.
- Use headings and lists to improve "skim-ability"
- Type your name at the bottom
- Include contact information when needed

The email contents:

To... message.recipient@email.com
Cc...
Bcc...
Subject: Concise, meaningful, professional subject line

Dear Message Recipient,

Emails are brief messages that can be quickly distributed to any size group of co-communicators. This message provides guidelines for appropriate email formatting.

Effective emails:

- Open with recipient name(s) and sometimes include a professional salutation
- Use left-aligned, single-spaced text for easy reading
- Add spaces between paragraphs for clarity
- Employ bulleted or numbered lists to allow for skimming
- Keep messages to one screen with attachments for longer messages
- Maintain direct, professional tone
- Close with the sender's name, information about who sent the message, and sometimes include a complimentary closing
- Do not contain confidential or sensitive information

Emails close with specific instructions or requests related to next steps. Please immediately begin to follow these tips for all professional emails that you send.

Best,

Email Guide

Email Guide, Ph.D.
Business Communication Professor
emailguide@email.com

Sections labeled: Intro, Body, Conclusion

are sometimes attached to emails due to the dissemin'
emails (e.g., free to send, can arrive at dispersed locatio'
If you wish to take advantage of these dissemination
ute a longer message, the text of your emails shoul/
the attached document. If you do not wish to atta'
your email, you should reconsider your choice of e.
ing in mind the one screen rule of thumb. Emails are u.
and memos in their length—though not necessarily their fo..
are a more formal channel of communication in organizations u.
believe them to be. Following grammar rules and formatting guidelines
Figure 8.1) will help your email communication to be viewed as competent.

To envision how the message considerations covered in Parts 1–3 might inform the construction of an email, let's return to the two meeting scenarios we discussed in Chapter 5. Recall that we wanted to inform our team of an upcoming meeting and persuade them to complete some work in advance of the meeting. Email was the preferred form of communication in your organization and was preferred for tasks like scheduling a meeting. In Scenario 1, your request that they complete their work prior to the meeting was unlikely to be met with any resistance because the project was clearly a top priority for everyone. Thus, you planned to take a direct approach to your email. Your email might look something like Figure 8.2. Note that the formatting preferences for email demonstrated in Figure 8.1 are present in this email example.

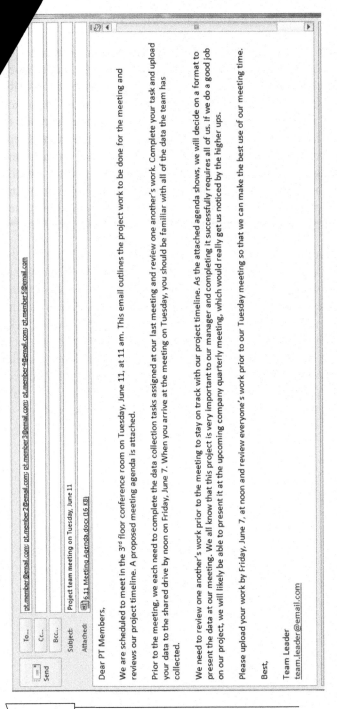

Figure 8.2 Example of email using direct approach.

The email shown reads:

To... pt.member@email.com; pt.member2@email.com; pt.member3@email.com; pt.member4@email.com; pt.member5@email.com
Cc...
Bcc...

Subject: Project team meeting on Tuesday, June 11

Attached: 6.11 Meeting Agenda.docx (16 KB)

Dear PT Members,

We are scheduled to meet in the 3rd floor conference room on Tuesday, June 11, at 11 am. This email outlines the project work to be done for the meeting and reviews our project timeline. A proposed meeting agenda is attached.

Prior to the meeting, we each need to complete the data collection tasks assigned at our last meeting and review one another's work. Complete your task and upload your data to the shared drive by noon on Friday, June 7. When you arrive at the meeting on Tuesday, you should be familiar with all of the data the team has collected.

We need to review one another's work prior to the meeting to stay on track with our project timeline. As the attached agenda shows, we will decide on a format to present the data at our meeting. We all know that this project is very important to our manager and completing it successfully requires all of us. If we do a good job on our project, we will likely be able to present it at the upcoming company quarterly meeting, which would really get us noticed by the higher ups.

Please upload your work by Friday, June 7, at noon and review everyone's work prior to our Tuesday meeting so that we can make the best use of our meeting time.

Best,

Team Leader
team.leader@email.com

In Scenario 2, your co-communicators were feeling pressed for time. Though this project is your priority, you are worried that your co-communicators might see it differently. You did not want to be too directive or critical of your team. So, you decided to take an indirect approach in your email. Figure 8.3 shows how the same request might look different in execution because of the SPACE. The key points covered are the same, but the organization of the email content differs. As with Figure 8.2, the formatting preferences for email remain the same in this example.

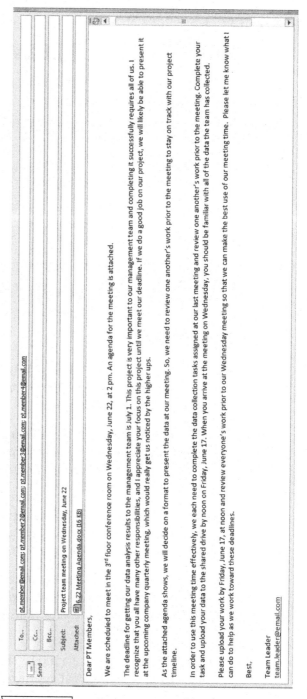

Dear PT Members,

We are scheduled to meet in the 3rd floor conference room on Wednesday, June 22, at 2 pm. An agenda for the meeting is attached.

The deadline for getting our data analysis results to the management team is July 1. This project is very important to our management team and completing it successfully requires all of us. I recognize that you all have many other responsibilities, and I appreciate your focus on this project until we meet our deadline. If we do a good job on our project, we will likely be able to present it at the upcoming company quarterly meeting, which would really get us noticed by the higher ups.

As the attached agenda shows, we will decide on a format to present the data at our meeting. So, we need to review one another's work prior to the meeting to stay on track with our project timeline.

In order to use this meeting time effectively, we each need to complete the data collection tasks assigned at our last meeting and review one another's work prior to the meeting. Complete your task and upload your data to the shared drive by noon on Friday, June 17. When you arrive at the meeting on Wednesday, you should be familiar with all of the data the team has collected.

Please upload your work by Friday, June 17, at noon and review everyone's work prior to our Wednesday meeting so that we can make the best use of our meeting time. Please let me know what I can do to help as we work toward these deadlines.

Best,

Team Leader
team.leader@email.com

To... pt.member@email.com; pt.member2@email.com; pt.member3@email.com; pt.member4@email.com

Cc...

Bcc...

Subject: Project team meeting on Wednesday, June 22

Attached: 6.22 Meeting Agenda.docx (16 KB)

Send

Figure 8.3 Example of email using indirect approach.

Key Chapter Takeaways

- Electronic media offer the ability to quickly disperse a message to any number of co-communicators.

- Confidential or sensitive information should never be communicated using electronic media.

- Use proper grammar, spelling, and punctuation as often as possible to facilitate shared meaning with your co-communicators.

- Adjust to limited nonverbal and verbal cues by paying careful attention to your word choice and use of cues like text and font choices, emoticons, and response times.

- Avoid multitasking, which leads to less competent communication.

- Work to maximize the benefits of the form of electronic media you use.

Endnotes

[1] Burgoon, J. K., & Walther, J. B. (2013). Media and computer mediation. In J. A. Hall & M. L. Knapp (Eds.) *Nonverbal communication* (pp. 731–770). Berlin, Germany: de Gruyter.

[2] Rubinstein, J. S., Meyer, D. E., & Evans, J. E. (2001). Executive control of cognitive processes in task switching. *Journal of Experimental Psychology: Human Perception and Performance, 27,* 763–797. doi: 10.1037//0096-1523.27.4.763

[3] Kirn, W. (2007, November 1). The autumn of the multitaskers. *The Atlantic.* Retrieved from http://www.theatlantic.com/magazine/archive/2007/11/the-autumn-of-the-multitaskers/306342/?single_page=true

[4] Foeher, U. G. (2006, December). *Media multitasking among American youth: Prevalence, predictors and pairings.* Retrieved from Kaiser Family Foundation website: http://kaiserfamilyfoundation.files.wordpress.com/2013/01/7592.pdf

[5] Stephens, K. K., & Davis, J. (2009). The social influences on electronic multitasking in organizational meetings. *Management Communication Quarterly, 23,* 62–83. doi: 10.1177/0893318909335417

[6] Kaplan, A. M., & Haenlein, M. (2010). Users of the world, unite! The challenges and opportunities of social media. *Business Horizons, 53*, 59–68. doi:10.1016/j.bushor.2009.09.003

[7] Blog.reppler.com (n.d.). *Managing your online image across social networks*. Retrieved from http://blog.reppler.com/2011/09/27/managing-your-online-image-across-social-networks/

[8] Findlay Schenck, B. (2013, June 4). 9 tips to power up your social media. *Entrepreneur*. Retrieved from http://www.entrepreneur.com/article/226891

[9] Joyner, A. (2010, January 25). 30 tips for using social media in your business. *Inc*. Retrieved from http://www.inc.com/articles/2010/01/30-tips-for-using-social-media.html

[10] Radicati, S., & Hoang, Q. (2011, May). *Email statistics report, 2011–2015*. Retrieved from The Radicati Group, Inc. website: http://www.radicati.com/wp/wp-content/uploads/2011/05/Email-Statistics-Report-2011-2015-Executive-Summary.pdf

[11] Chui, M., Manyika, J., Bughin, J., Dobbs, R., Roxburgh, C., Sarrazin, J., & Westergren, M. (2012, July). *The social economy: Unlocking value and productivity through social technologies*. Retrieved from the McKinsey & Company website: http://www.mckinsey.com/insights/high_tech_telecoms_internet/the_social_economy?p=1

Chapter 9

Communication Competence in Traditional Written Media

When to Use Traditional Written Media

Traditional written forms of media (here limited to letters, memos, and reports) are well-established formats for disseminating information in organizations. Traditional written media are less interactive than either oral or electronic forms of media. They are ideal when

- a permanent record is needed
- a high level of detail is required
- formality is required or appropriate

These general guidelines apply to all forms of traditional written media. Of course, different forms of traditional written media also offer different strengths and should be used in different contexts.

Ideal SPACE		
Letter	**Memo**	**Report**
Usually addressed to a single co-communicator	Can be shared with any number of co-communicators	Can be shared with any number of co-communicators
More personalized content appropriate	Message does not require personalization to specific co-communicators	Typically incorporates other visual elements, such as charts or graphs
Correspondence that typically expects response or is in response to another message	Response from co-communicators not expected	Includes formulaic aspects, like table of contents/bookmarks and executive summary to help co-communicators navigate a lengthy document
Can be for internal or external co-communicators	Internal co-communicators	Can be for internal or external co-communicators
Typically does not exceed two pages in length	Typically does not exceed three pages in length	Longer than three pages

Encoding/Decoding Skills of Special Interest

Using the encoding/decoding framework discussed in Chapter 2, we will explore how competent communicators can use and attend to these cues. Because written output is comparatively permanent and static, following the frameworks laid out in this text (i.e., SPACE and SAID) to carefully analyze, develop, and evaluate (ADE) your message is especially important. Ultimately, effective workplace writing relies on a series of contextual decisions[1] for producing your written message.

Language Use and Clear Verbal Expression

This concern is almost synonymous with traditional written communication. Much attention is paid to proper word choice, grammatically clean writing, correct punctuation, clear argument focus, and organization because your co-communicators can take as much time as they wish with a written document and can even reference it later. Further, you can spend ample time revising drafts to make your document strong in all areas. Though certainly applicable to other forms of media, some particular issues around language use and clear verbal expression are worth highlighting in this section. Correct and concise language is particularly important because your message is not easily revised once disseminated.

In the revising and evaluating stage, we make modifications to our message that improve verbal expression. Most people think strictly about proofreading for grammatical errors and typos at this stage. Indeed, business message readers are distracted by basic sentence-structure errors such as run-ons, fragments, nonparallel structure and misuse of commas, apostrophes (e.g., its vs. it's or improper possessives), and other punctuation.[2] For help with grammar, word choice, punctuation, subject–verb agreement, and other nitty-gritty issues, you should supplement this text with a grammar text. Because our focus here is more on structure, we will attend to: (1) sentence structure; (2) active vs. passive voice; (3) people-centered messages; and (4) a process for revision to improve clarity, correctness, and conciseness at the sentence level.

Sentence Structure

In Chapter 5, a framework for structuring paragraphs (the house method) was introduced. The building blocks for a paragraph are, of course, sentences. Sentences are complete when they have a verb and a noun (which may be unwritten) and make sense on their own. Clauses also contain a verb. Usually, clauses are parts of sentences, but they may also be sentences themselves depending on the type of clause. *Independent* or *main* clauses can stand alone. *Dependent* or *subordinate* clauses rely on independent clauses for their meaning. Finally, *phrases* are groups of related words within a clause.[3] Clauses and phrases work to form sentences. For example, the following sentence consists of an **independent or main clause**, a dependent or subordinate clause, *and two phrases*.

In the afternoon, **most employees meet** *in project teams* when they can.

Depending on the combination of clauses used, we can form sentences of different types and complexities. Let's talk about four sentence types here:

1. **Simple sentence** (one independent clause)
   Our low entry-level salaries reduce our organization's profits every year.

2. **Compound sentence** (two independent clauses)
   Performance review data shows that internally promoted managers receive higher average ratings, and teams supervised by internally promoted managers average more per month in sales.

3. **Complex sentence** (one independent and one dependent clause)
   Because both general performance and sales numbers are important indicators of managers' performance, internally promoted managers are on average better performers than externally hired managers.

4. **Compound–complex sentence** (at least two independent clauses and one dependent clause)
   Though comparative costs of turnover are difficult to calculate, the higher turnover rate for externally hired managers coupled with the increased costs for hiring them has high costs for our organization; recruiting strong entry-level candidates and promoting them into sales manager roles creates stability in these important positions.

Because conciseness is a standard for competent business communications, you should work to reduce compound–complex sentences in your writing. Often, these sentences can be rephrased or re-punctuated to become simple, compound, or complex sentences. Identifying and questioning the use of compound–complex sentences is a fairly straightforward way to improve conciseness in your writing.

Active vs. Passive Voice

Having built sentences, we need to understand how we can better use sentences to meet our goals and demonstrate understanding of our co-communicators. A distinguishing characteristic of a sentence is the presence of a verb. Verbs can be either active (e.g., communicated) or passive (e.g., were communicated). The nature of the verb used in the sentence is labeled "active voice" or "passive voice." In active voice, the subject of the sentence is the "doer" of the action. In passive voice, the subject is either part of a subordinate clause (usually following the verb) or is left unspecified. Passive voice focuses attention on the action rather than on a person or persons, so it can be more tactful.

- Active voice: I recommend that we increase entry-level salaries.

- Passive voice: A case can be made for increasing entry-level salaries.

Still uncertain about whether you are using active or passive voice? Professor Rebecca Johnson[4] offers a fun guideline to tell the difference: *If your sentence makes sense when you add the phrase "by zombies" after the verb, your sentence has passive voice.* For example:

- Active voice: I recommend [by zombies] that we increase entry-level salaries.

- Passive voice: A case can be made [by zombies] for increasing entry-level salaries.

Often, we are told to use only active voice in professional writing. Active voice is more direct; it eliminates extra words. Active voice also improves clarity by directly linking an action to the "doer" of the action. However, active voice is not always best. The choice between active and passive voice is informed by the SPACE. Specifically, if you have decided that a direct approach is appropriate for your message, active voice is preferable. Conversely, if you have decided to use an indirect approach, then use of passive voice to make sensitive points or contested claims is appropriate. During your revision and evaluation of your messages, you should attend to whether you have used active or passive voice and which would be most appropriate given your goals and co-communicators. Most people prefer consistency in the use of active or passive voice, so make sure you are consistent in choosing one.

People-Centered Messages (at the Sentence Level)

Using active or passive voice based on your direct or indirect approach is just one way to demonstrate your focus on your co-communicators. You can also use certain phrasing. You have analyzed what should be SAID, so you can emphasize your understanding of your co-communicators' needs in your phrasing. For example:

- I need you to send your complete credit card information so that I can process your order. (me centered)
- Your order will be sent upon receipt of your complete credit card information. (people centered)

In your revision and evaluation, ask yourself whether you are taking an expressive approach (saying what you think) rather than constructing a creative message that helps your goals be realized while addressing your co-communicators' needs (a rhetorical approach).

A Process for Revising Sentences

At this point, you have worked so hard constructing and revising your sentences that the idea of cutting anything is difficult. (This affection for what we have written is one reason why peer review is a helpful step on the path to clear, concise prose.) One approach that you can take to distance yourself from your writing is the Paramedic Method.[5] You or others can use this popular editing technique to streamline your writing. Follow the steps of the Paramedic Method to improve the readability of your sentences. For each sentence in the document:

1. Underline the prepositions (e.g., at, on, of, in, about, for, onto, into).
2. Circle the "to be" verb forms (e.g., am, is, are, was, were, be, being).
3. Box the action.
4. Change the "action" into a simple, active verb (if active voice is desired).
5. Make the "doer" of the action the sentence's subject (if active voice is desired).
6. Eliminate any unnecessary clauses or modifiers, prepositional phrases, or redundancies in language.

Appropriate Nonverbal Communication

Like some forms of electronic media, traditional written media are particularly "lean" forms of media (see the chart in Chapter 4). These forms of media can offer more verbal cues because longer messages are acceptable. However, nonverbal cues are in some ways more limited than the forms of electronic media discussed in Chapter 8. From the extensive list of nonverbal cues we have been using, only two are pertinent.

- Physical characteristics: Standard formats are typically followed for letters, memos, and reports. Though the organization for which you work might have its own preferred formats, many are standardized across organizations. Following one of these accepted formats cues your co-communicators in to the type of message you are sending. Further, following these formats allows your co-communicators to quickly locate information they need because locations are standardized in the formatting. These formats arrange information in ways that are accessible to your co-communicators (helping your communication to be people centered). Figures 9.1 and 9.2 provide guides for block letter formatting and memo formatting, respectively.

- Paravocalics: Your co-communicators will look to textual cues to provide the information about stress or emphasis that we normally get through tone. The font you use sends a message on its own! Be sure to use professional, readable fonts to convey appropriate tone. Use italics, underlining, or bold font to emphasize particular things—like your key points or claims. Such cues take the place of other forms of paravocalics and help your co-communicators to interpret your message.

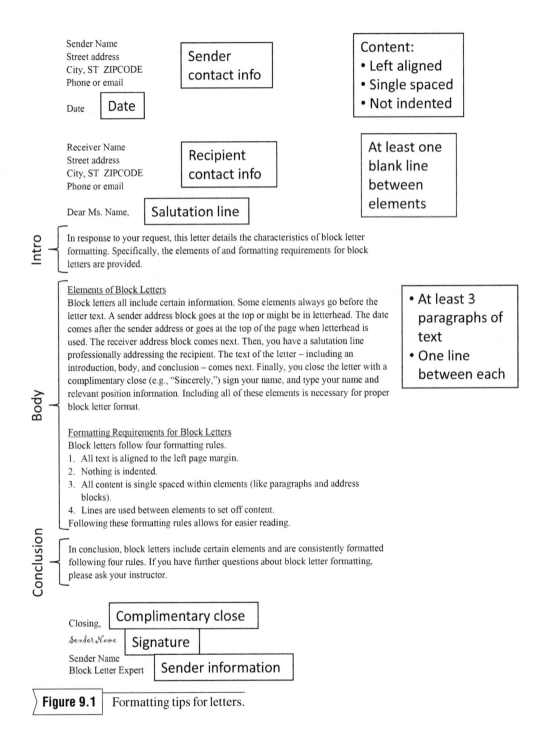

Sender Name
Street address
City, ST ZIPCODE
Phone or email

Date **Date**

Sender contact info

Content:
• Left aligned
• Single spaced
• Not indented

Receiver Name
Street address
City, ST ZIPCODE
Phone or email

Recipient contact info

At least one blank line between elements

Dear Ms. Name, **Salutation line**

Intro

In response to your request, this letter details the characteristics of block letter formatting. Specifically, the elements of and formatting requirements for block letters are provided.

Body

Elements of Block Letters
Block letters all include certain information. Some elements always go before the letter text. A sender address block goes at the top or might be in letterhead. The date comes after the sender address or goes at the top of the page when letterhead is used. The receiver address block comes next. Then, you have a salutation line professionally addressing the recipient. The text of the letter – including an introduction, body, and conclusion – comes next. Finally, you close the letter with a complimentary close (e.g., "Sincerely,") sign your name, and type your name and relevant position information. Including all of these elements is necessary for proper block letter format.

• At least 3 paragraphs of text
• One line between each

Formatting Requirements for Block Letters
Block letters follow four formatting rules.
1. All text is aligned to the left page margin.
2. Nothing is indented.
3. All content is single spaced within elements (like paragraphs and address blocks).
4. Lines are used between elements to set off content.
Following these formatting rules allows for easier reading.

Conclusion

In conclusion, block letters include certain elements and are consistently formatted following four rules. If you have further questions about block letter formatting, please ask your instructor.

Closing, **Complimentary close**
Sender Name **Signature**
Sender Name
Block Letter Expert **Sender information**

Figure 9.1 Formatting tips for letters.

Heading

Date:	Month #, YEAR
To:	Names of Co-Communicator(s)
From:	Your Name, Relevant Role
Subject:	Concise, meaningful, professional subject line

Use tab settings to align heading information

Intro

When formatting memos for internal distribution, certain guidelines should be followed. The elements of and formatting requirements for memos are provided below.

Body

Elements of Memos
Memos all include certain information. The heading at the top of the sheet always includes the date ("Date"), to whom the memo will be distributed ("To"), who wrote the memo ("From), and a descriptive subject line ("Subject"). The text includes an introduction, body, and conclusion. A clear preview sentence in the introduction outlines the content of the memo using the exact terms used in either the headings or body paragraph topic sentences. Consistently phrased and formatted headings in the body can help co-communicators locate pertinent information. Finally, a conclusion summarizes key information. Including all of these elements is necessary for proper memo format.

- At least 3 paragraphs of text
- One blank line between elements

Formatting Requirements for Memos
Memos follow four formatting rules.
1. All text is aligned to the left page margin.
2. Nothing is indented.
3. All content is single spaced within paragraphs.
4. Lines are used between elements to set off content.
Following these formatting rules allows for easier reading.

Content:
- Left aligned
- Single spaced
- Not indented

Conclusion

In conclusion, memos include certain elements and are consistently formatted following four rules. If you have further questions about memo formatting, please ask your instructor.

IF USED: Headings consistently formatted; only for body paragraphs

Figure 9.2 Formatting tips for memos.

Interpretation and the Ability to Respond Appropriately

Because the SPACE model situates your co-communicators' concerns as central to achieving your goals, evaluating others' reactions to your message is part of being a competent communicator. Figures 9.3 and 9.4 show how a message (specifically, a memo) might differ based on SPACE considerations. Revisiting the recommendation to increase entry-level salaries example from Chapter 5, these memos show different approaches suitable for two different communication SPACEs. In both scenarios, your instrumental goal is the same. You want to propose increasing salaries for entry-level positions and support that recommendation with three pieces of evidence: (1) your company's entry-level salaries are lower than competitors' entry-level salaries, (2) internally promoted employees are better performers than those externally hired for upper-level roles, and (3) employees who enter through entry-level roles and are promoted are less likely to leave. You believe this evidence supports your recommendation because attracting and retaining good entry-level employees is important to your organization, and raising entry-level salaries would address both issues. Memos are the typical format for presenting recommendations in your organization, so you in this case decide to write a memo. You aim to present accurate information (correct and ethical) in a concise manner.

To envision how the message considerations covered in Parts 1–3 might inform this memo, let's walk through two scenarios so that you can see how everything comes together to produce a written document. In Scenario 1, imagine that your manager approaches you. She tells you that she feels like your organization's entry-level salaries are too low and asks you to put together a case she can present in favor of increasing them. Because your manager requested you make this recommendation, you know the direct approach is appropriate. In this SPACE, your memo would look something like Figure 9.3. In Scenario 2, you have been analyzing data about staffing and salaries as part of your work in human resources. Based on this analysis, you know that your organization's entry-level salaries are too low and that increasing them would address several issues with which the organization is struggling. Because you know that budgets are always tight and your manager will carefully evaluate your argument, you decide to take an indirect approach that logically builds to your recommendation. In this SPACE, your memo would look something like Figure 9.4. In looking at these two messages, you see that the information presented is nearly identical. However, the order differs. You can identify the necessary components of direct and indirect messages in both examples.

Date: April 10, 2015

To: Sandra Garcia, Human Resources Director

From: Pat Johnson, Human Resources Assistant

Subject: Proposal for entry-level salary increases

Our low entry-level salaries reduce our organization's profits every year. Increasing entry-level salaries would not only reduce costs but would also benefit our company in other ways. To support the case for entry-level salary increases, I outline market salary data, summarize comparative performance data for internally promoted vs. externally hired managers, and highlight turnover rates for internally promoted vs. externally hired managers.

Market Salary Data
Salaries for our entry-level employees lag behind those of our competitors. Our starting salary for entry-level sales assistants is $30,000. A Salary.com comparison shows that this salary is significantly lower than both local and national markets. In the local market, sales assistants at companies of comparable size have a median starting salary of $36,020. Our salaries are also below the national median of $35,236. This gap is considerably wider than it was a few years ago. Our comparatively low salaries cost us in the market. In the last year, 42% of our campus-recruiting candidates accepted another offer. These rejections lead to increased recruiting costs and might be costing us the best candidates. Comparable salaries for these roles would help us to continue to attract the best entry-level candidates.

Comparative Performance of Internally Promoted vs. Externally Hired Managers
Two key performance indicators show that employees who are internally promoted are better performers. First, an analysis of performance review data from the last five years shows that internally promoted managers receive an average rating of 4.3 (which translates to "Good" in our rating scale), while externally hired managers receive an average rating of 3.5 (which translates to "Average" in our scale). Second, teams supervised by internally promoted managers average $9,073 more per month in sales. Because both general performance and sales numbers are important indicators of manager performance, internally promoted managers are on average better performers than externally hired managers. Attracting and retaining entry-level employees, some of whom will eventually become internally promoted managers, is key to our company's continued success.

Turnover Rates for Internally Promoted vs. Externally Hired Managers
Attracting good entry-level employees and promoting them into sales manager roles also reduces turnover. An analysis of turnover rates for the last five years shows that externally hired sales managers were twice as likely to leave the company. In addition, external hires cost more than internal promotions. Though the comparative costs of these employees leaving the organization are difficult to calculate, logic dictates that the higher turnover rate for externally hired managers coupled with the increased costs for hiring them has high costs for our organization. Recruiting strong entry-level candidates and promoting them into sales manager roles creates stability in these important positions.

In conclusion, attracting and retaining good entry-level employees is important to the organization. Higher entry-level salaries would help us do both. Increasing entry-level salaries will make us more competitive in the marketplace. Hiring the best candidates into these positions is key because when they are promoted into sales manager positions they are better performers who are less likely to leave the company. In short, increasing entry-level salaries saves us money by increasing our sales and performance while decreasing our turnover costs.

> **Figure 9.3** | Example of memo using direct approach

Date: April 10, 2015

To: Sam Garcia, Human Resources Director

From: Pat Johnson, Human Resources Assistant

Subject: Proposal for entry-level salary increases

When our entry-level employees are promoted into sales manager positions they are better performers who are less likely to leave the company compared to externally hired managers. Thus, we need to focus on attracting and retaining good entry-level employees. Below I provide the results of my recent staffing analysis focused on our sales function.

Comparative Performance of Internally Promoted vs. Externally Hired Managers
Two key performance indicators show that internally promoted employees are better performers. First, an analysis of performance review data from the last five years shows that internally promoted managers receive an average rating of 4.3 (which translates to "Good" in our rating scale), while externally hired managers receive an average rating of 3.5 (which translates to "Average" in our scale). Second, teams supervised by internally promoted managers average $9,073 more per month in sales. Because both general performance and sales numbers are important indicators of manager performance, internally promoted managers are on average better performers than externally hired managers. Attracting and retaining entry-level employees, some of whom will eventually become internally promoted managers, is key to our company's continued success.

Turnover Rates for Internally Promoted vs. Externally Hired Managers
Attracting good entry-level employees and promoting them into sales manager roles also reduces turnover. An analysis of turnover rates for the last five years shows that externally hired sales managers were twice as likely to leave the company. In addition, external hires cost more than internal promotions. Though the comparative costs of these employees leaving the organization are difficult to calculate, logic dictates that the higher turnover rate for externally hired managers coupled with the increased costs for hiring them has high costs for our organization. Recruiting strong entry-level candidates and promoting them into sales manager roles creates stability in these important positions.

Market Salary Data
Hiring the best candidates into entry-level sales assistant positions is key because when they are promoted into sales manager positions they are better performers who are less likely to leave the company. However, salaries for our entry-level employees lag behind those of our competitors. Our starting salary for entry-level sales assistants is $30,000. A Salary.com comparison shows that this salary is significantly lower than both local and national markets. In the local market, sales assistants at comparably-sized companies have a median starting salary of $36,020. Our salaries are also below the national median of $35, 236. This gap is considerably wider than it was a few years ago. Our comparatively low salaries cost us in the market. In the last year, 42% of our campus-recruiting candidates accepted another offer. These rejections lead to increased recruiting costs and might be costing us the best candidates. Increasing entry-level salaries will make us more competitive in the marketplace and continue to attract the best candidates.

In conclusion, attracting and retaining strong entry-level employees is important to the organization. Higher entry-level salaries would help us do both. Though the initial concern might be that the company lacks money to raise entry-level employee salaries, the reduction in our company turnover costs will more than cover the difference. In short, increasing entry-level salaries saves us money by increasing our sales and performance while decreasing our turnover costs. Our low entry-level salaries reduce our organization's profits every year. Increasing entry-level salaries would not only reduce costs but would also benefit our company in other ways.

> **Figure 9.4** | Example of memo using indirect approach.

When writing workplace messages using traditional written media, employees often go through multiple versions of a message, making changes based on co-communicator feedback. Often, the most important co-communicator in workplace writing is your manager. Though what one manager sees as competent writing may be quite different from the expectations of another,[1] some findings point to general considerations. In general, managers and executives view the following as most important when evaluating written communication: wordiness, format, organization, audience, grammar/proofreading, vocabulary or word choice, inclusion of relevant details and/or facts, argument structure, and clarity.[6] This list reminds us that simply proofreading a message is not sufficient to be perceived as a competent communicator. We need to look both at the sentence structure/grammatical level and at the macro level (e.g., logical flow, goal achievement, and audience focus) when revising our writing.[7]

To a certain extent, however, you will learn to write on the job and for a particular manager co-communicator. To learn in this setting, employees often co-write documents, seek colleague opinions on written products, discuss approaches to writing, and share documents with one another to provide guidance on writing.[8] What is expected or perceived as competent on a specific team in a specific organizational context is learned through these exchanges. Reading other's work also helps to improve writing,[9] so reading the writing of your colleagues and manager(s) is a smart way to improve your own writing.

Of course, the frameworks provided in this book actually point you toward this kind of process. You have been encouraged to consider multiple types of goals, your co-communicators, organizational norms for appropriateness, expectations for correctness and conciseness, and ethical considerations. Working to understand a specific co-communicator's (i.e., manager's) preferences for writing easily fits into this SPACE.

Key Chapter Takeaways

- Traditional written media are formal methods of communication that establish a permanent record.

- Correct and concise language is particularly important in traditional written media because they are less interactive than other forms of media and can be referenced repeatedly by co-communicators.

- Revise multiple drafts of written messages, attending to your sentence structure and voice while checking for grammatical issues and typing errors.

- Use the Paramedic Method[5] to improve clarity and conciseness.

- Evaluate your drafts with concern for your co-communicators at both the (micro) sentence/verb tense level and (macro) argument and content level.

- Adjust to limited nonverbal cues by paying careful attention to your formatting, structure, word choice, and use of cues like text and font choices.

- On the job, pay careful attention to what is appropriate or preferred for certain co-communicators.

- Learn by reading other's writing and working collaboratively on drafts.

Endnotes

[1] Brizee, A. (2012, April 17). *Paramedic Method: A lesson in writing concisely.* Retrieved from the Purdue OWL website: https://owl.english.purdue.edu/owl/resource/635/01/

[2] Gilsdorf, J., & Leonard, D. (2001). Big stuff, little stuff: A decennial measurement of executives' and academics' reactions to questionable usage elements. *Journal of Business Communication, 38,* 439–475. doi: 0.1177/002194360103800403

[3] Oxforddictionaries.com. (n.d.). Sentences, clauses, and phrases. In Oxford Dictionaries. Retrieved from http://www.oxforddictionaries.com/words/sentences-clauses-and-phrases

[4] Johnson, R. [johnsonr]. (2012, October 18). I finally learned how to teach my guys to ID the passive voice. If you can insert "by zombies" after the verb, you have passive voice. Retrieved from https://twitter.com/johnsonr/status/259012668298506240

[5] Lantham, R. (2006). *Revising prose.* London: Longman.

[6] Feinberg, S., & Pritzker, I. (1985). An MBA communications course designed by business executives. *Journal of Business Communication, 22,* 75–83. doi: 10.1177/002194368502200410

[7] Roundy, N. (1983). A program for revision in business and technical writing. *Journal of Business Communication, 20,* 55–66. doi: 10.1177/002194368302000106

[8] Rogers, P. S., Ho, M. L., Thomas, J., Wong, I. F. H., & Chang, C. O. L. (2004). Preparing new entrants for subordinate reporting: A decision-making framework for writing. *Journal of Business Communication, 41*, 370–401. doi: 10.1177/0021943604268442

[9] Gieselman, R. D. (1982). Reading, writing, and research: Pedagogical implications. *Journal of Business Communication, 19*, 23–38. doi: 10.1177/002194368201900402

Appendix: Worksheets

This appendix contains worksheets for in-class work that complement the text. Multiple copies of each worksheet are provided. Here is an overview of the worksheets provided:

- Goal Worksheet
- SAID Worksheet
- Media Choices Worksheet
- Key Points Worksheet
- Resource Evaluation Worksheet
- Structure Worksheet
- House Worksheet
- Argument Worksheet
- Message Evaluation Worksheet
- SPACE Model for Competent Communication

Name _Samuel Cetnaro_

Goal Worksheet: Use this worksheet to specify your instrumental, relational, and self-presentation goals for a communicative task.

1. What specific action, response, outcome, and/or resource are you trying to obtain through your communication?

   Friendship

   1(a). Circle one: Is your instrumental goal primarily *persuasive* or *informative*?

2. Are you trying to develop, maintain, or end a relationship with your co-communicator(s)?

   Develop

3. How do you want your co-communicator(s) to ⌐ ⌐ou? How do you wish to present yourself?

   In a friendly manner.

Name _____

Goal Worksheet: Use this worksheet to specify your instrumental, relational, and self-presentation goals for a communicative task.

1. What specific action, response, outcome, and/or resource are you trying to obtain through your communication?

    1(a). Circle one: Is your instrumental goal primarily *persuasive* or *informative*?

2. Are you trying to develop, maintain, or end a relationship with your co-communicator(s)?

3. How do you want your co-communicator(s) to see you? How do you wish to present yourself?

Name _____

Goal Worksheet: Use this worksheet to specify your instrumental, relational, and self-presentation goals for a communicative task.

1. What specific action, response, outcome, and/or resource are you trying to obtain through your communication?

    1(a). Circle one: Is your instrumental goal primarily *persuasive* or *informative*?

2. Are you trying to develop, maintain, or end a relationship with your co-communicator(s)?

3. How do you want your co-communicator(s) to see you? How do you wish to present yourself?

Name Sam Cetnaro

SAID Worksheet: Use this worksheet to analyze your co-communicator(s).

1. With whom are you directly communicating?

    Sarah Cairoli

2. Who else might see your communication?

    Her staff, other students

3. What should be SAID to your co-communicator(s)?

    Situation: What are your co-communicator(s)' goals? To better the BBcc.

    Instrumental: Helpful with the goal,

    Relational: Graded on helpfulness

    Self-Presentation: Knowledge

    How do your goals relate to those of your co-communicator(s)?

    Grade dependent on Big Idea challenge

    How receptive will your co-communicator(s) be to your goals? Somewhat, if the idea is worthwhile,

    Are there any threats to your co-communicator(s)' sense of control or self-esteem in this situation?

    Possibly, I've never met Sarah,

Attitudes: How might your co-communicator(s) feel about the message you have to convey?

Greatful

Does your message threaten your co-communicator(s)' sense of control or their self-esteem?

Possibly, if its a good idea,

What opinions will your co-communicator(s) already have about the situation?

That the PBCC is a great plan for learning

How might your co-communicator(s) respond to your message?

Happy

Information: What does your co-communicator/do your co-communicators already know?

Everything

What information do you need to provide?

Something differt

What misinformation will you have to correct?

Only needs use BBC

Demographics: What is/are your co-communicator(s) like? How might that affect how you choose to communicate with them?

Teachers, I need to [?]

Where is/are your co-communicator(s) located?

Downstairs

If you have multiple targeted co-communicators, how much diversity in attitudes and information is there?

Name _____

SAID Worksheet: Use this worksheet to analyze your co-communicator(s).

   1. With whom are you directly communicating?

   2. Who else might see your communication?

   3. What should be SAID to your co-communicator(s)?

   Situation: What are your co-communicator(s)' goals?

        Instrumental:

        Relational:

        Self-Presentation:

        How do your goals relate to those of your
        co-communicator(s)?

        How receptive will your co-communicator(s) be to your
        goals?

        Are there any threats to your co-communicator(s)' sense
        of control or self-esteem in this situation?

Attitudes: How might your co-communicator(s) feel about the message you have to convey?

Does your message threaten your co-communicator(s)' sense of control or their self-esteem?

What opinions will your co-communicator(s) already have about the situation?

How might your co-communicator(s) respond to your message?

Information: What does your co-communicator/do your co-communicators already know?

What information do you need to provide?

What misinformation will you have to correct?

Demographics: What is/are your co-communicator(s) like? How might that affect how you choose to communicate with them?

Where is/are your co-communicator(s) located?

If you have multiple targeted co-communicators, how much diversity in attitudes and information is there?

Name _____

SAID Worksheet: Use this worksheet to analyze your co-communicator(s).

1. With whom are you directly communicating?

2. Who else might see your communication?

3. What should be SAID to your co-communicator(s)?

   Situation: What are your co-communicator(s)' goals?

   Instrumental:

   Relational:

   Self-Presentation:

   How do your goals relate to those of your
   co-communicator(s)?

   How receptive will your co-communicator(s) be to your
   goals?

   Are there any threats to your co-communicator(s)' sense
   of control or self-esteem in this situation?

Attitudes: How might your co-communicator(s) feel about the message you have to convey?

Does your message threaten your co-communicator(s)' sense of control or their self-esteem?

What opinions will your co-communicator(s) already have about the situation?

How might your co-communicator(s) respond to your message?

Information: What does your co-communicator/do your co-communicators already know?

What information do you need to provide?

What misinformation will you have to correct?

Demographics: What is/are your co-communicator(s) like? How might that affect how you choose to communicate with them?

Where is/are your co-communicator(s) located?

If you have multiple targeted co-communicators, how much diversity in attitudes and information is there?

Name _____

Media Choices Worksheet: Use this worksheet to analyze your media choices.

Is the message you need to send (check all that apply):

☐ Ambiguous/open to interpretation? *If yes, richer media (e.g., oral media) are preferable.*

☐ Confidential? *If yes, do not use electronic media.*

☐ Requiring documentation? *If yes, do not use only oral media.*

☐ Time sensitive? *If yes, electronic or oral media are preferable.*

☐ Lengthy? *If yes, written media might be preferable.*

Given the nature of the message, your strategy, the people involved, and the organizational context, what medium/media would be most appropriate and why?

What conventions should you follow given the medium/media you have chosen?

Turn over for detailed information about different forms of media →

Channel	Medium	Level of Verbal Detail (Length)	Nonverbal Cues Available	Number of Co-Communicators	Asynchronous?	Level of Privacy	Permanence	Interaction Speed/ Immediacy	"Redo" Capability
Traditional Written *Best when:* • Permanent record needed • High level of detail required • Formality desired	Letter	1–2 pages	Appearance, Tone	Small (1)	Yes	Mod	High	Slow	High
	Memo	< 3 pages	Appearance, Tone	Varies	Yes	Mod	High	Slow	High
	Report	> 3 pages	Appearance, Tone	Varies	Yes	Mod	High	Slow	High
Electronic *Best when:* • Message needs to be delivered quickly • Privacy is not required • Level of detail needed is low • Feedback is desired, but immediacy is less important	Text message	1 screen	Type Cues (e.g., font, emoticons)	Small	Yes/ No	Low/ Mod	Mod	Varies	Mod
	Email	1 screen	Appearance, Tone, Type Cues	Varies	Yes	Low	High	Varies	High
	Internet	1 screen	Varies	Varies	Yes	Low	High-Mod	Varies	High
	Social media	Varies	Varies	Varies	Yes/ No	Low	High	Varies	High
Oral *Best when:* • Message requires rich cues, immediate feedback • No permanent record needed • Interaction can be synchronous • Message can be delivered without need to edit	Phone call	Varies	Paravocalics	Small	No	High	Low	Fast	Low
	Presentation	Varies	Kinesics, Appearance, Proxemics, Paravocalics, Chronemics	Varies	No	Mod	Varies	Mod	Low
	Group meeting	Varies	Kinesics, Appearance, Proxemics, Paravocalics, Chronemics	Mod (3–10)	No	Mod	Varies	Fast	Low
	Video Conference	Varies	Kinesics, Appearance, Paravocalics, Chronemics	Small	No	High	Low	Fast	Low
	Face-to-face conversation	Varies	Kinesics, Appearance, Proxemics, Paravocalics, Chronemics	Small (1)	No	High	Low	Fast	Low

Name _____

Media Choices Worksheet: Use this worksheet to analyze your media choices.

Is the message you need to send (check all that apply):

- ☐ Ambiguous/open to interpretation? *If yes, richer media (e.g., oral media) are preferable.*

- ☐ Confidential? *If yes, do not use electronic media.*

- ☐ Requiring documentation? *If yes, do not use only oral media.*

- ☐ Time sensitive? *If yes, electronic or oral media are preferable.*

- ☐ Lengthy? *If yes, written media might be preferable.*

Given the nature of the message, your strategy, the people involved, and the organizational context, what medium/media would be most appropriate and why?

What conventions should you follow given the medium/media you have chosen?

Turn over for detailed information about different forms of media →

Channel	Medium	Level of Verbal Detail (Length)	Nonverbal Cues Available	Number of Co-Communicators	Asynchronous?	Level of Privacy	Permanence	Interaction Speed/ Immediacy	"Redo" Capability
Traditional Written *Best when:* • Permanent record needed • High level of detail required • Formality desired	Letter	1–2 pages	Appearance, Tone	Small (1)	Yes	Mod	High	Slow	High
	Memo	< 3 pages	Appearance, Tone	Varies	Yes	Mod	High	Slow	High
	Report	> 3 pages	Appearance, Tone	Varies	Yes	Mod	High	Slow	High
Electronic *Best when:* • Message needs to be delivered quickly • Privacy is not required • Level of detail needed is low • Feedback is desired, but immediacy is less important	Text message	1 screen	Type Cues (e.g., font, emoticons)	Small	Yes/No	Low/Mod	Mod	Varies	Mod
	Email	1 screen	Appearance, Tone, Type Cues	Varies	Yes	Low	High	Varies	High
	Internet	1 screen	Varies	Varies	Yes	Low	High-Mod	Varies	High
	Social media	Varies	Varies	Varies	Yes/No	Low	High	Varies	High
Oral *Best when:* • Message requires rich cues, immediate feedback • No permanent record needed • Interaction can be synchronous • Message can be delivered without need to edit	Phone call	Varies	Paravocalics	Small	No	High	Low	Fast	Low
	Presentation	Varies	Kinesics, Appearance, Proxemics, Paravocalics, Chronemics	Varies	No	Mod	Varies	Mod	Low
	Group meeting	Varies	Kinesics, Appearance, Proxemics, Paravocalics, Chronemics	Mod (3–10)	No	Mod	Varies	Fast	Low
	Video Conference	Varies	Kinesics, Appearance, Paravocalics, Chronemics	Small	No	High	Low	Fast	Low
	Face-to-face conversation	Varies	Kinesics, Appearance, Proxemics, Paravocalics, Chronemics	Small (1)	No	High	Low	Fast	Low

Name _____

Media Choices Worksheet: Use this worksheet to analyze your media choices.

Is the message you need to send (check all that apply):

☐ Ambiguous/open to interpretation? *If yes, richer media (e.g., oral media) are preferable.*

☐ Confidential? *If yes, do not use electronic media.*

☐ Requiring documentation? *If yes, do not use only oral media.*

☐ Time sensitive? *If yes, electronic or oral media are preferable.*

☐ Lengthy? *If yes, written media might be preferable.*

Given the nature of the message, your strategy, the people involved, and the organizational context, what medium/media would be most appropriate and why?

What conventions should you follow given the medium/media you have chosen?

Turn over for detailed information about different forms of media →

Channel	Medium	Level of Verbal Detail (Length)	Nonverbal Cues Available	Number of Co-Communicators	Asynchronous?	Level of Privacy	Permanence	Interaction Speed/ Immediacy	"Redo" Capability
Traditional Written *Best when:* • Permanent record needed • High level of detail required • Formality desired	Letter	1–2 pages	Appearance, Tone	Small (1)	Yes	Mod	High	Slow	High
	Memo	< 3 pages	Appearance, Tone	Varies	Yes	Mod	High	Slow	High
	Report	> 3 pages	Appearance, Tone	Varies	Yes	Mod	High	Slow	High
Electronic *Best when:* • Message needs to be delivered quickly • Privacy is not required • Level of detail needed is low • Feedback is desired, but immediacy is less important	Text message	1 screen	Type Cues (e.g., font, emoticons)	Small	Yes/ No	Low/ Mod	Mod	Varies	Mod
	Email	1 screen	Appearance, Tone, Type Cues	Varies	Yes	Low	High	Varies	High
	Internet	1 screen	Varies	Varies	Yes	Low	High-Mod	Varies	High
	Social media	Varies	Varies	Varies	Yes/ No	Low	High	Varies	High
Oral *Best when:* • Message requires rich cues, immediate feedback • No permanent record needed • Interaction can be synchronous • Message can be delivered without need to edit	Phone call	Varies	Paravocalics	Small	No	High	Low	Fast	Low
	Presentation	Varies	Kinesics, Appearance, Proxemics, Paravocalics, Chronemics	Varies	No	Mod	Varies	Mod	Low
	Group meeting	Varies	Kinesics, Appearance, Proxemics, Paravocalics, Chronemics	Mod (3–10)	No	Mod	Varies	Fast	Low
	Video Conference	Varies	Kinesics, Appearance, Paravocalics, Chronemics	Small	No	High	Low	Fast	Low
	Face-to-face conversation	Varies	Kinesics, Appearance, Proxemics, Paravocalics, Chronemics	Small (1)	No	High	Low	Fast	Low

Name _____

Key Points Worksheet: Use this worksheet to identify your key points.

1. Translate your instrumental goal into a topic statement or claim.

2. What key points do you need to make to reach your instrumental, relational, and self-presentation goals? In other words, what information does/do your co-communicator(s) need to know for you to accomplish your goals?

Name _____

Key Points Worksheet: Use this worksheet to identify your key points.

1. Translate your instrumental goal into a topic statement or claim.

2. What key points do you need to make to reach your instrumental, relational, and self-presentation goals? In other words, what information does/do your co-communicator(s) need to know for you to accomplish your goals?

Name _____

Key Points Worksheet: Use this worksheet to identify your key points.

1. Translate your instrumental goal into a topic statement or claim.

2. What key points do you need to make to reach your instrumental, relational, and self-presentation goals? In other words, what information does/do your co-communicator(s) need to know for you to accomplish your goals?

Name _____

Key Points Worksheet: Use this worksheet to identify your key points.

1. Translate your instrumental goal into a topic statement or claim.

2. What key points do you need to make to reach your instrumental, relational, and self-presentation goals? In other words, what information does/do your co-communicator(s) need to know for you to accomplish your goals?

Name _____

Resource Evaluation Worksheet: Use this worksheet to evaluate the resources you gather to support your key points.

Source 1:

    A. Authority: Does this person/group know what they are talking about? How do you know?

    B. Bias: Is the source objective? Is it all opinion or are there facts? How do you know?

    C. Content: How is the information useful or relevant to my topic/claim?

    C. Currency: Is the information timely?

Source 2:

    A. Authority: Does this person/group know what they are talking about? How do you know?

    B. Bias: Is the source objective? Is it all opinion or are there facts? How do you know?

    C. Content: How is the information useful or relevant to my topic/claim?

    C. Currency: Is the information timely?

Source 3:

    A. Authority: Does this person/group know what they are talking about? How do you know?

    B. Bias: Is the source objective? Is it all opinion or are there facts? How do you know?

    C. Content: How is the information useful or relevant to my topic/claim?

    C. Currency: Is the information timely?

Source 4:

    A. Authority: Does this person/group know what they are talking about? How do you know?

    B. Bias: Is the source objective? Is it all opinion or are there facts? How do you know?

    C. Content: How is the information useful or relevant to my topic/claim?

    C. Currency: Is the information timely?

Name _____

Resource Evaluation Worksheet: Use this worksheet to evaluate the resources you gather to support your key points.

Source 1:

    A. Authority: Does this person/group know what they are talking about? How do you know?

    B. Bias: Is the source objective? Is it all opinion or are there facts? How do you know?

    C. Content: How is the information useful or relevant to my topic/claim?

    C. Currency: Is the information timely?

Source 2:

    A. Authority: Does this person/group know what they are talking about? How do you know?

    B. Bias: Is the source objective? Is it all opinion or are there facts? How do you know?

    C. Content: How is the information useful or relevant to my topic/claim?

    C. Currency: Is the information timely?

Source 3:

    A. Authority: Does this person/group know what they are talking about? How do you know?

    B. Bias: Is the source objective? Is it all opinion or are there facts? How do you know?

    C. Content: How is the information useful or relevant to my topic/claim?

    C. Currency: Is the information timely?

Source 4:

    A. Authority: Does this person/group know what they are talking about? How do you know?

    B. Bias: Is the source objective? Is it all opinion or are there facts? How do you know?

    C. Content: How is the information useful or relevant to my topic/claim?

    C. Currency: Is the information timely?

Name _____

Resource Evaluation Worksheet: Use this worksheet to evaluate the resources you gather to support your key points.

Source 1:

    A. Authority: Does this person/group know what they are talking about? How do you know?

    B. Bias: Is the source objective? Is it all opinion or are there facts? How do you know?

    C. Content: How is the information useful or relevant to my topic/claim?

    C. Currency: Is the information timely?

Source 2:

    A. Authority: Does this person/group know what they are talking about? How do you know?

    B. Bias: Is the source objective? Is it all opinion or are there facts? How do you know?

    C. Content: How is the information useful or relevant to my topic/claim?

    C. Currency: Is the information timely?

Source 3:

   A. Authority: Does this person/group know what they are talking about? How do you know?

   B. Bias: Is the source objective? Is it all opinion or are there facts? How do you know?

   C. Content: How is the information useful or relevant to my topic/claim?

   C. Currency: Is the information timely?

Source 4:

   A. Authority: Does this person/group know what they are talking about? How do you know?

   B. Bias: Is the source objective? Is it all opinion or are there facts? How do you know?

   C. Content: How is the information useful or relevant to my topic/claim?

   C. Currency: Is the information timely?

Name _____

Resource Evaluation Worksheet: Use this worksheet to evaluate the resources you gather to support your key points.

Source 1:

    A. Authority: Does this person/group know what they are talking about? How do you know?

    B. Bias: Is the source objective? Is it all opinion or are there facts? How do you know?

    C. Content: How is the information useful or relevant to my topic/claim?

    C. Currency: Is the information timely?

Source 2:

    A. Authority: Does this person/group know what they are talking about? How do you know?

    B. Bias: Is the source objective? Is it all opinion or are there facts? How do you know?

    C. Content: How is the information useful or relevant to my topic/claim?

    C. Currency: Is the information timely?

Source 3:

    A. Authority: Does this person/group know what they are talking about? How do you know?

    B. Bias: Is the source objective? Is it all opinion or are there facts? How do you know?

    C. Content: How is the information useful or relevant to my topic/claim?

    C. Currency: Is the information timely?

Source 4:

    A. Authority: Does this person/group know what they are talking about? How do you know?

    B. Bias: Is the source objective? Is it all opinion or are there facts? How do you know?

    C. Content: How is the information useful or relevant to my topic/claim?

    C. Currency: Is the information timely?

Name _____

Structure Worksheet: Use this worksheet to outline your structure.

Would your strategy and co-communicator(s) be best served by a direct or indirect approach? Will your co-communicator(s):

☐ Agree with or be unopposed to the information/argument you present?

☐ Prefer a direct approach?

☐ Be likely to overlook your key points if not presented directly?

☐ Feel that their self-esteem is not affected by your key points?

☐ Feel that their sense of autonomy or choice is not affected by your key points?

Responses in this column suggest that a direct approach is appropriate.

☐ Disagree with or be opposed to the information/argument you present?

☐ Be presented with a logical argument that builds to your recommendation, key point, or goal?

☐ Be likely to devote time and focus to your message?

☐ Feel that their self-esteem is threatened by your key points?

☐ Feel that their sense of autonomy or choice is threatened by your key points?

Responses in this column suggest that an indirect approach is appropriate.

Evaluate your responses and make the choice that seems most appropriate given the context.
A direct argument will present the main point right away.
An indirect argument will build to the main point after presenting the argument.

Given the direct or indirect approach you plan to take, what should go in the **introduction**?

Attention Getter or Context:

Topic Statement:

Preview Statement (for direct approach only):

What key points do you need to cover in the body? (See Key Points Worksheet.)

- In what order should your key points be addressed to be effective in achieving your goals? (Number them in the list above.)
- What content/evidence (e.g., sources) can you use to support each key point? (Identify them in the list above.)
- What ties the content/evidence you identified to each point (i.e., the warrant)? (Add them to the list above.)

What should go in the **conclusion**?

Name _____

Structure Worksheet: Use this worksheet to outline your structure.

Would your strategy and co-communicator(s) be best served by a direct or indirect approach? Will your co-communicator(s):

☐ Agree with or be unopposed to the information/argument you present?	☐ Disagree with or be opposed to the information/argument you present?
☐ Prefer a direct approach?	☐ Be presented with a logical argument that builds to your recommendation, key point, or goal?
☐ Be likely to overlook your key points if not presented directly?	☐ Be likely to devote time and focus to your message?
☐ Feel that their self-esteem is not affected by your key points?	☐ Feel that their self-esteem is threatened by your key points?
☐ Feel that their sense of autonomy or choice is not affected by your key points?	☐ Feel that their sense of autonomy or choice is threatened by your key points?
Responses in this column suggest that a direct approach is appropriate.	Responses in this column suggest that an indirect approach is appropriate.

Evaluate your responses and make the choice that seems most appropriate given the context.
A direct argument will present the main point right away.
An indirect argument will build to the main point after presenting the argument.

Given the direct or indirect approach you plan to take, what should go in the **introduction**?

Attention Getter or Context:

Topic Statement:

Preview Statement (for direct approach only):

What key points do you need to cover in the body? (See Key Points Worksheet.)

- In what order should your key points be addressed to be effective in achieving your goals? (Number them in the list above.)
- What content/evidence (e.g., sources) can you use to support each key point? (Identify them in the list above.)
- What ties the content/evidence you identified to each point (i.e., the warrant)? (Add them to the list above.)

What should go in the **conclusion**?

Name _____

Structure Worksheet: Use this worksheet to outline your structure.

Would your strategy and co-communicator(s) be best served by a direct or indirect approach? Will your co-communicator(s):

☐ Agree with or be unopposed to the information/argument you present?

☐ Disagree with or be opposed to the information/argument you present?

☐ Prefer a direct approach?

☐ Be presented with a logical argument that builds to your recommendation, key point, or goal?

☐ Be likely to overlook your key points if not presented directly?

☐ Be likely to devote time and focus to your message?

☐ Feel that their self-esteem is not affected by your key points?

☐ Feel that their self-esteem is threatened by your key points?

☐ Feel that their sense of autonomy or choice is not affected by your key points?

☐ Feel that their sense of autonomy or choice is threatened by your key points?

Responses in this column suggest that a direct approach is appropriate.

Responses in this column suggest that an indirect approach is appropriate.

Evaluate your responses and make the choice that seems most appropriate given the context.
A direct argument will present the main point right away.
An indirect argument will build to the main point after presenting the argument.

Given the direct or indirect approach you plan to take, what should go in the **introduction**?

Attention Getter or Context:

Topic Statement:

Preview Statement (for direct approach only):

What key points do you need to cover in the body? (See Key Points Worksheet.)

- In what order should your key points be addressed to be effective in achieving your goals? (Number them in the list above.)
- What content/evidence (e.g., sources) can you use to support each key point? (Identify them in the list above.)
- What ties the content/evidence you identified to each point (i.e., the warrant)? (Add them to the list above.)

What should go in the **conclusion**?

Name _____

Structure Worksheet: Use this worksheet to outline your structure.

Would your strategy and co-communicator(s) be best served by a direct or indirect approach? Will your co-communicator(s):

☐ Agree with or be unopposed to the information/argument you present?

☐ Prefer a direct approach?

☐ Be likely to overlook your key points if not presented directly?

☐ Feel that their self-esteem is not affected by your key points?

☐ Feel that their sense of autonomy or choice is not affected by your key points?

Responses in this column suggest that a direct approach is appropriate.

☐ Disagree with or be opposed to the information/argument you present?

☐ Be presented with a logical argument that builds to your recommendation, key point, or goal?

☐ Be likely to devote time and focus to your message?

☐ Feel that their self-esteem is threatened by your key points?

☐ Feel that their sense of autonomy or choice is threatened by your key points?

Responses in this column suggest that an indirect approach is appropriate.

Evaluate your responses and make the choice that seems most appropriate given the context.
A direct argument will present the main point right away.
An indirect argument will build to the main point after presenting the argument.

Given the direct or indirect approach you plan to take, what should go in the **introduction**?

Attention Getter or Context:

Topic Statement:

Preview Statement (for direct approach only):

What key points do you need to cover in the body? (See Key Points Worksheet.)

- In what order should your key points be addressed to be effective in achieving your goals? (Number them in the list above.)
- What content/evidence (e.g., sources) can you use to support each key point? (Identify them in the list above.)
- What ties the content/evidence you identified to each point (i.e., the warrant)? (Add them to the list above.)

What should go in the **conclusion**?

Name _____

House Worksheet: Build a house for each body paragraph/section. Make sure the topic of each paragraph/section relates to your message's topic statement/claim and is explicitly introduced in your preview statement (for direct messages).

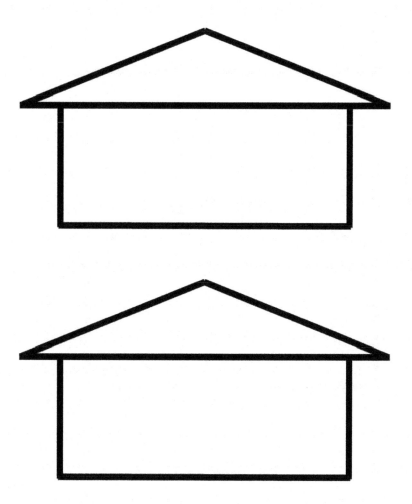

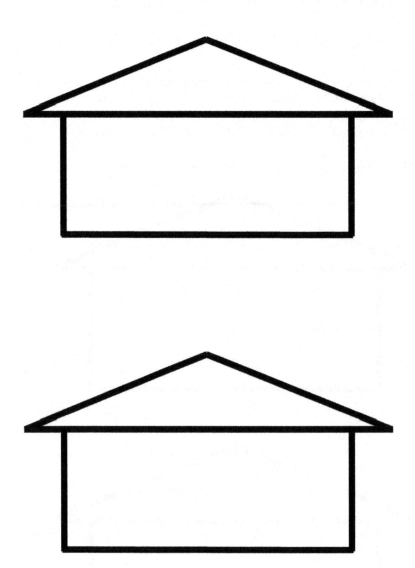

Name _____

House Worksheet: Build a house for each body paragraph/section. Make sure the topic of each paragraph/section relates to your message's topic statement/claim and is explicitly introduced in your preview statement (for direct messages).

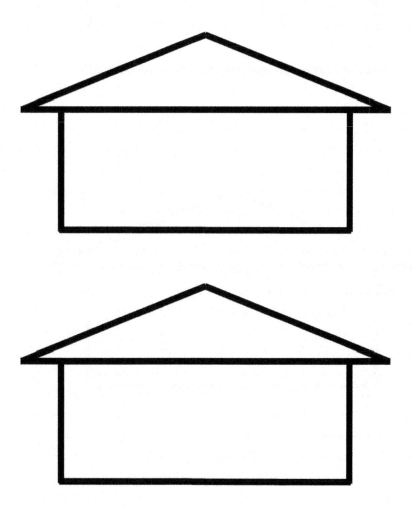

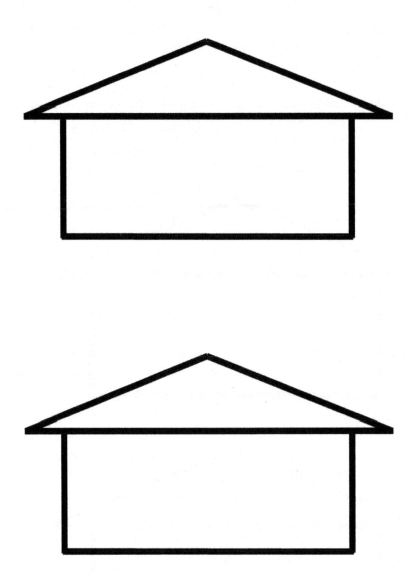

Name _____

House Worksheet: Build a house for each body paragraph/section. Make sure the topic of each paragraph/section relates to your message's topic statement/claim and is explicitly introduced in your preview statement (for direct messages).

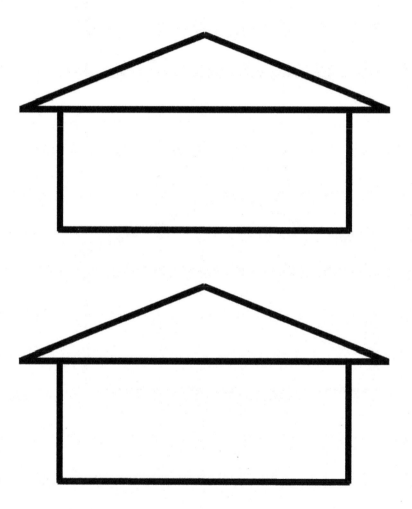

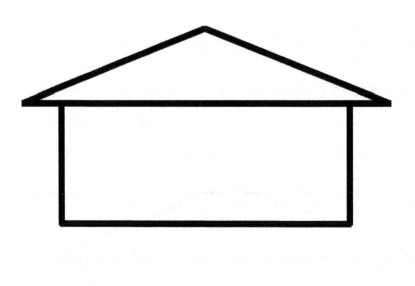

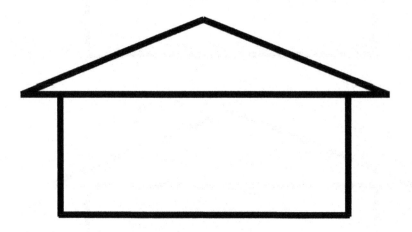

Name _____

House Worksheet: Build a house for each body paragraph/section. Make sure the topic of each paragraph/section relates to your message's topic statement/claim and is explicitly introduced in your preview statement (for direct messages).

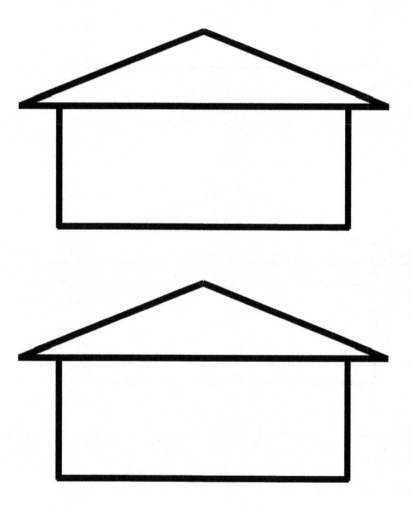

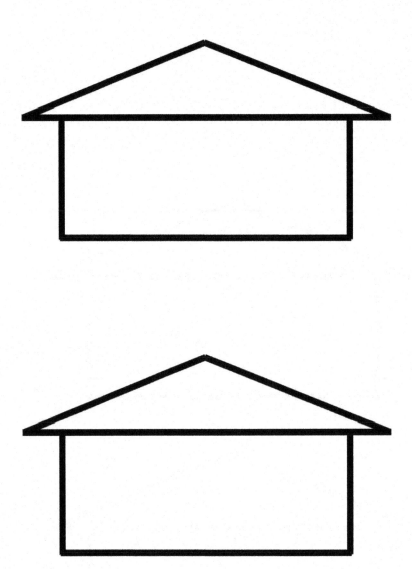

Name _____

Argument Worksheet: Use this worksheet to develop two-sided refutational arguments.

List your key points here (see Key Points Worksheet).	List counter-arguments for each key point here.	List refutations for each counter-argument here.

List your key points here (see Key Points Worksheet).	List counter-arguments for each key point here.	List refutations for each counter-argument here.

Name _____

Argument Worksheet: Use this worksheet to develop two-sided refutational arguments.

List your key points here (see Key Points Worksheet).	List counter-arguments for each key point here.	List refutations for each counter-argument here.

List your key points here (see Key Points Worksheet).	List counter-arguments for each key point here.	List refutations for each counter-argument here.

Name _____

Argument Worksheet: Use this worksheet to develop two-sided refutational arguments.

List your key points here (see Key Points Worksheet).	List counter-arguments for each key point here.	List refutations for each counter-argument here.

List your key points here (see Key Points Worksheet).	List counter-arguments for each key point here.	List refutations for each counter-argument here.

Name _____

Message Evaluation Worksheet: Use this worksheet to evaluate messages.

S. Y / N Is the message successful in achieving its instrumental, relational, and self-presentation goals?

    Y / N Are the key points needed to be effective in achieving the message's goals addressed?

    Y / N Does the message consistently follow the house structure at the macro and micro levels to make a strong argument?

If you answered "no" to any of these questions, what should be changed?

P. How will this message be viewed by targeted and secondary co-communicators?

Situation: Y / N Does the message focus on co-communicators' needs?

                Y / N Does the message recognize co-communicators' goals?

                Y / N Will co-communicators be receptive to this message?

If you answered "no" to any of these questions, what should be changed?

Attitudes: Y / N Does this message reflect an understanding of co-communicators' feelings?

                Y / N Does this message show an understanding of co-communicators' opinions?

                Y / N Does this message anticipate and address potential responses?

If you answered "no" to any of these questions, what should be changed?

Information: Y / N Does this message provide all information needed by co-communicators?

                Y / N Does this message correct misinformation in a respectful manner?

If you answered "no" to either question, what should be changed?

Demographics: Does this message address the particular concerns related to co-communicator preferences, locations, and diversity? If not, what should be changed?

A. Y / N   Given the nature of the message, strategy, and people involved, does the message seem appropriate in terms of the medium used?

Y / N   Given the nature of the message, strategy, and people involved, does the message seem appropriate in terms of the information provided?

Y / N   Do the ABCs of the primary and secondary sources make the sources appropriate for inclusion?

Y / N   Does the message have a clear introduction, body, and conclusion with appropriate information included in each one given the approach taken?

Y / N   Given the nature of the message, strategy, and people involved, does the message seem appropriate in terms of the message strategies (i.e., direct vs. indirect approach, message sidedness) used?

If you answered "no" to any of these questions, what should be changed?

C. Y / N   Is the formatting correct based on the conventions of the medium used?

Y / N   Is the information vital to achieving instrumental, relational, and self-presentation goals presented?

Y / N   Is the information presented concisely? (For written messages, use the Paramedic Method to streamline writing.)

Y / N   Are sources presented and cited correctly?

Y / N   For written messages, is the text free of grammatical, word choice, or language errors?

If you answered "no" to any of these questions, what should be fixed?

E.   Do you feel this is the right way to approach the situation? Why or why not?

If this message were disseminated to a much wider (even nonbusiness audience), how would they view it?

Name _____

Message Evaluation Worksheet: Use this worksheet to evaluate messages.

S. Y / N   Is the message successful in achieving its instrumental, relational, and self-presentation goals?

    Y / N   Are the key points needed to be effective in achieving the message's goals addressed?

    Y / N   Does the message consistently follow the house structure at the macro and micro levels to make a strong argument?

If you answered "no" to any of these questions, what should be changed?

P. How will this message be viewed by targeted and secondary co-communicators?

    Situation: Y / N   Does the message focus on co-communicators' needs?

                  Y / N   Does the message recognize co-communicators' goals?

                  Y / N   Will co-communicators be receptive to this message?

                If you answered "no" to any of these questions, what should be changed?

    Attitudes: Y / N   Does this message reflect an understanding of co-communicators' feelings?

                  Y / N   Does this message show an understanding of co-communicators' opinions?

                  Y / N   Does this message anticipate and address potential responses?

                If you answered "no" to any of these questions, what should be changed?

    Information: Y / N   Does this message provide all information needed by co-communicators?

                  Y / N   Does this message correct misinformation in a respectful manner?

If you answered "no" to either question, what should be changed?

Demographics: Does this message address the particular concerns related to co-communicator preferences, locations, and diversity? If not, what should be changed?

A. Y / N   Given the nature of the message, strategy, and people involved, does the message seem appropriate in terms of the medium used?

Y / N   Given the nature of the message, strategy, and people involved, does the message seem appropriate in terms of the information provided?

Y / N   Do the ABCs of the primary and secondary sources make the sources appropriate for inclusion?

Y / N   Does the message have a clear introduction, body, and conclusion with appropriate information included in each one given the approach taken?

Y / N   Given the nature of the message, strategy, and people involved, does the message seem appropriate in terms of the message strategies (i.e., direct vs. indirect approach, message sidedness) used?

If you answered "no" to any of these questions, what should be changed?

C. Y / N   Is the formatting correct based on the conventions of the medium used?

Y / N   Is only information vital to achieving instrumental, relational, and self-presentation goals presented?

Y / N   Is the information presented concisely? (For written messages, use the Paramedic Method to streamline writing.)

Y / N   Are sources presented and cited correctly?

Y / N   For written messages, is the text free of grammatical, word choice, or language errors?

If you answered "no" to any of these questions, what should be fixed?

E. Do you feel this is the right way to approach the situation? Why or why not?

If this message were disseminated to a much wider (even non-business audience), how would they view it?

Name _____

Message Evaluation Worksheet: Use this worksheet to evaluate messages.

S. Y / N   Is the message successful in achieving its instrumental, relational, and self-presentation goals?

    Y / N   Are the key points needed to be effective in achieving the message's goals addressed?

    Y / N   Does the message consistently follow the house structure at the macro and micro levels to make a strong argument?

If you answered "no" to any of these questions, what should be changed?

P. How will this message be viewed by targeted and secondary co-communicators?

Situation: Y / N   Does the message focus on co-communicators' needs?

                Y / N   Does the message recognize co-communicators' goals?

                Y / N   Will co-communicators be receptive to this message?

If you answered "no" to any of these questions, what should be changed?

Attitudes: Y / N   Does this message reflect an understanding of co-communicators' feelings?

                Y / N   Does this message show an understanding of co-communicators' opinions?

                Y / N   Does this message anticipate and address potential responses?

If you answered "no" to any of these questions, what should be changed?

Information: Y / N   Does this message provide all information needed by co-communicators?

                Y / N   Does this message correct misinformation in a respectful manner?

If you answered "no" to either question, what should be changed?

Demographics: Does this message address the particular concerns related to co-communicator preferences, locations, and diversity? If not, what should be changed?

A. Y / N   Given the nature of the message, strategy, and people involved, does the message seem appropriate in terms of the medium used?

Y / N   Given the nature of the message, strategy, and people involved, does the message seem appropriate in terms of the information provided?

Y / N   Do the ABCs of the primary and secondary sources make the sources appropriate for inclusion?

Y / N   Does the message have a clear introduction, body, and conclusion with appropriate information included in each one given the approach taken?

Y / N   Given the nature of the message, strategy, and people involved, does the message seem appropriate in terms of the message strategies (i.e., direct vs. indirect approach, message sidedness) used?

If you answered "no" to any of these questions, what should be changed?

C. Y / N   Is the formatting correct based on the conventions of the medium used?

Y / N   Is only information vital to achieving instrumental, relational, and self-presentation goals presented?

Y / N   Is the information presented concisely? (For written messages, use the Paramedic Method to streamline writing.)

Y / N   Are sources presented and cited correctly?

Y / N   For written messages, is the text free of grammatical, word choice, or language errors?

If you answered "no" to any of these questions, what should be fixed?

E.   Do you feel this is the right way to approach the situation? Why or why not?

If this message were disseminated to a much wider (even non-business audience), how would they view it?

Name _____

Message Evaluation Worksheet: Use this worksheet to evaluate messages.

S.   Y / N   Is the message successful in achieving its instrumental, relational, and self-presentation goals?

     Y / N   Are the key points needed to be effective in achieving the message's goals addressed?

     Y / N   Does the message consistently follow the house structure at the macro and micro levels to make a strong argument?

If you answered "no" to any of these questions, what should be changed?

P.   How will this message be viewed by targeted and secondary co-communicators?

Situation: Y / N   Does the message focus on co-communicators' needs?

             Y / N   Does the message recognize co-communicators' goals?

             Y / N   Will co-communicators be receptive to this message?

If you answered "no" to any of these questions, what should be changed?

Attitudes: Y / N   Does this message reflect an understanding of co-communicators' feelings?

             Y / N   Does this message show an understanding of co-communicators' opinions?

             Y / N   Does this message anticipate and address potential responses?

If you answered "no" to any of these questions, what should be changed?

Information: Y / N   Does this message provide all information needed by co-communicators?

             Y / N   Does this message correct misinformation in a respectful manner?

If you answered "no" to either question, what should be changed?

Demographics: Does this message address the particular concerns related to co-communicator preferences, locations, and diversity? If not, what should be changed?

A. Y / N   Given the nature of the message, strategy, and people involved, does the message seem appropriate in terms of the medium used?

Y / N   Given the nature of the message, strategy, and people involved, does the message seem appropriate in terms of the information provided?

Y / N   Do the ABCs of the primary and secondary sources make the sources appropriate for inclusion?

Y / N   Does the message have a clear introduction, body, and conclusion with appropriate information included in each one given the approach taken?

Y / N   Given the nature of the message, strategy, and people involved, does the message seem appropriate in terms of the message strategies (i.e., direct vs. indirect approach, message sidedness) used?

If you answered "no" to any of these questions, what should be changed?

C. Y / N   Is the formatting correct based on the conventions of the medium used?

Y / N   Is only information vital to achieving instrumental, relational, and self-presentation goals presented?

Y / N   Is the information presented concisely? (For written messages, use the Paramedic Method to streamline writing.)

Y / N   Are sources presented and cited correctly?

Y / N   For written messages, is the text free of grammatical, word choice, or language errors?

If you answered "no" to any of these questions, what should be fixed?

E. Do you feel this is the right way to approach the situation? Why or why not?

If this message were disseminated to a much wider (even non-business audience), how would they view it?

SPACE Model for Competent Communication

	Strategic	People-Focused	Appropriate	Correct & Concise	Ethical
Concept	Focused on goals	Concerned with co-communicators and their perspective	Uses acceptable medium to present professional message in logical manner	Follows standards to present succinct, focused message	Takes implications of message for all co-communicators into account
Considerations for Planning	What specific action, response, outcome, and/or resource are you trying to obtain through your communication? Is that goal primarily persuasive or informative? Are you trying to develop, maintain, or end a relationship with your co-communicator(s)? How do you want your co-communicator(s) to see you? How do you wish to present yourself?	With whom are you communicating? What should be SAID to your co-communicator(s)? Who else might see your communication?	Is the message you need to send: ambiguous/open to interpretation, confidential, requiring documentation, time sensitive, or lengthy? Given the nature of the message, your strategy, the people involved, and the organizational context, what medium would be most appropriate? Would your strategy and co-communicators be best served by a direct or indirect approach?	What conventions should you follow given the medium you have chosen? What information is vital and what could be removed?	What do you feel is the ethical way to approach the situation?
Considerations for Evaluating	Can you identify the message's goals? How successful is the message in achieving those goals? Are the key points needed to be effective in achieving the message's goals addressed? Does the message consistently follow the house structure at the macro and micro levels to make a strong argument?	How will this message be viewed by targeted and secondary co-communicators? What is SAID?	Given the nature of the message, strategy, and the people involved, does the message seem appropriate in terms of the medium used and the information provided? Do the ABCs of the primary and secondary sources make them appropriate for inclusion? Does the message have a clear introduction, body, and conclusion with appropriate information included in each one given the approach taken? Given the nature of the message, strategy, and the people involved, does the message seem appropriate in terms of the message strategies (i.e., direct vs. indirect approach, message sidedness) used?	Is the message correct? Is the formatting correct based on the conventions of the medium used? What information is vital and what could be removed? Is the information presented concisely? Are sources cited correctly? Are there any grammatical, word choice, or language errors?	Do you feel this is the right way to approach the situation? If this message were disseminated to a much wider (even non-business audience), how would they view it?

SPACE Model for Competent Communication

	Strategic	People-Focused	Appropriate	Correct & Concise	Ethical
Concept	Focused on goals	Concerned with co-communicators and their perspective	Uses acceptable medium to present professional message in logical manner	Follows standards to present succinct, focused message	Takes implications of message for all co-communicators into account
Considerations for Planning	What specific action, response, outcome, and/or resource are you trying to obtain through your communication? Is that goal primarily persuasive or informative? Are you trying to develop, maintain, or end a relationship with your co-communicator(s)? How do you want your co-communicator(s) to see you? How do you wish to present yourself?	With whom are you communicating? What should be SAID to your co-communicator(s)? Who else might see your communication?	Is the message you need to send: ambiguous/open to interpretation, confidential, requiring documentation, time sensitive, or lengthy? Given the nature of the message, your strategy, the people involved, and the organizational context, what medium would be most appropriate? Would your strategy and co-communicators be best served by a direct or indirect approach?	What conventions should you follow given the medium you have chosen? What information is vital and what could be removed?	What do you feel is the ethical way to approach the situation?
Considerations for Evaluating	Can you identify the message's goals? How successful is the message in achieving those goals? Are the key points needed to be effective in achieving the message's goals addressed? Does the message consistently follow the house structure at the macro and micro levels to make a strong argument?	How will this message be viewed by targeted and secondary co-communicators? What is SAID?	Given the nature of the message, strategy, and the people involved, does the message seem appropriate in terms of the medium used and the information provided? Do the ABCs of the primary and secondary sources make them appropriate for inclusion? Does the message have a clear introduction, body, and conclusion with appropriate information included in each one given the approach taken? Given the nature of the message, strategy, and the people involved, does the message seem appropriate in terms of the message strategies (i.e., direct vs. indirect approach, message sidedness) used?	Is the message correct? Is the formatting correct based on the conventions of the medium used? What information is vital and what could be removed? Is the information presented concisely? Are sources cited correctly? Are there any grammatical, word choice, or language errors?	Do you feel this is the right way to approach the situation? If this message were disseminated to a much wider (even non-business audience), how would they view it?

SPACE Model for Competent Communication				
	Strategic	**People-Focused**	**Appropriate**	**Correct & Concise**	**Ethical**

	Strategic	**People-Focused**	**Appropriate**	**Correct & Concise**	**Ethical**
Concept	Focused on goals	Concerned with co-communicators and their perspective	Uses acceptable medium to present professional message in logical manner	Follows standards to present succinct, focused message	Takes implications of message for all co-communicators into account
Considerations for Planning	What specific action, response, outcome, and/or resource are you trying to obtain through your communication? Is that goal primarily persuasive or informative? Are you trying to develop, maintain, or end a relationship with your co-communicator(s)? How do you want your co-communicator(s) to see you? How do you wish to present yourself?	With whom are you communicating? What should be SAID to your co-communicator(s)? Who else might see your communication?	Is the message you need to send: ambiguous/open to interpretation, confidential, requiring documentation, time sensitive, or lengthy? Given the nature of the message, your strategy, the people involved, and the organizational context, what medium would be most appropriate? Would your strategy and co-communicators be best served by a direct or indirect approach?	What conventions should you follow given the medium you have chosen? What information is vital and what could be removed?	What do you feel is the ethical way to approach the situation?
Considerations for Evaluating	Can you identify the message's goals? How successful is the message in achieving those goals? Are the key points needed to be effective in achieving the message's goals addressed? Does the message consistently follow the house structure at the macro and micro levels to make a strong argument?	How will this message be viewed by targeted and secondary co-communicators? What is SAID?	Given the nature of the message, strategy, and the people involved, does the message seem appropriate in terms of the medium used and the information provided? Do the ABCs of the primary and secondary sources make them appropriate for inclusion? Does the message have a clear introduction, body, and conclusion with appropriate information included in each one given the approach taken? Given the nature of the message, strategy, and the people involved, does the message seem appropriate in terms of the message strategies (i.e., direct vs. indirect approach, message sidedness) used?	Is the message correct? Is the formatting correct based on the conventions of the medium used? What information is vital and what could be removed? Is the information presented concisely? Are sources cited correctly? Are there any grammatical, word choice, or language errors?	Do you feel this is the right way to approach the situation? If this message were disseminated to a much wider (even non-business audience), how would they view it?

SPACE Model for Competent Communication				
Strategic	**People-Focused**	**Appropriate**	**Correct & Concise**	**Ethical**
Concept Focused on goals	Concerned with co-communicators and their perspective	Uses acceptable medium to present professional message in logical manner	Follows standards to present succinct, focused message	Takes implications of message for all co-communicators into account
Considerations for Planning What specific action, response, outcome, and/or resource are you trying to obtain through your communication? Is that goal primarily persuasive or informative? Are you trying to develop, maintain, or end a relationship with your co-communicator(s)? How do you want your co-communicator(s) to see you? How do you wish to present yourself?	With whom are you communicating? What should be SAID to your co-communicator(s)? Who else might see your communication?	Is the message you need to send: ambiguous/open to interpretation, confidential, requiring documentation, time sensitive, or lengthy? Given the nature of the message, your strategy, the people involved, and the organizational context, what medium would be most appropriate? Would your strategy and co-communicators be best served by a direct or indirect approach?	What conventions should you follow given the medium you have chosen? What information is vital and what could be removed?	What do you feel is the ethical way to approach the situation?
Considerations for Evaluating Can you identify the message's goals? How successful is the message in achieving those goals? Are the key points needed to be effective in achieving the message's goals addressed? Does the message consistently follow the house structure at the macro and micro levels to make a strong argument?	How will this message be viewed by targeted and secondary co-communicators? What is SAID?	Given the nature of the message, strategy, and the people involved, does the message seem appropriate in terms of the medium used and the information provided? Do the ABCs of the primary and secondary sources make them appropriate for inclusion? Does the message have a clear introduction, body, and conclusion with appropriate information included in each one given the approach taken? Given the nature of the message, strategy, and the people involved, does the message seem appropriate in terms of the message strategies (i.e., direct vs. indirect approach, message sidedness) used?	Is the message correct? Is the formatting correct based on the conventions of the medium used? What information is vital and what could be removed? Is the information presented concisely? Are sources cited correctly? Are there any grammatical, word choice, or language errors?	Do you feel this is the right way to approach the situation? If this message were disseminated to a much wider (even non-business audience), how would they view it?

CPSIA information can be obtained
at www.ICGtesting.com
Printed in the USA
LVOW02s1604091116
511933LV00003B/4/P